Beyond Stick Control

FOR THE SNARE AND DRUM SET PLAYER

by Glenn W. Meyer

Progressive Approaches to Snare Drum Rudiments

Features:
- **Hand Technique Development**
- **Hand/Foot Development**
- **Ostinato Foot Pattern Development**
- **Linear Jazz Studies**
- **Contains 8 bar solos for:**
  - **Rudiments**
  - **Two sound level accenting**
  - **Coordination**

CD contents

1. Opening Solo and Dialogue
2. Part A Hand Technique Development; Part B Hand/Foot Development; 8 Bar Solos Using 8th Note Rhythms (pp. 7-18)
3. 8 Bar Solos Using Triplet Rhythms: Parts A and B (pp. 19-24)
4. 8 Bar Solos Using 8th Notes and Triplets: Parts A and B (pp. 25-26)
5. 8 Bar Solos Using 16th Note Rhythms: Parts A and B (pp. 27-29)
6. Ostinato Foot Pattern Development: Part C; 8 Bar Solos Using 8th Note Rhythms (pp. 30-41)
7. 8 Bar Solos Using Triplet Rhythms: Part C (pp. 42-47)
8. 8 Bar Solos Using 16th Note Rhythms: Part C (pp. 48-50)
9. Linear Jazz Style: Part D (pp. 51-60)

1 2 3 4 5 6 7 8 9 0

EXCLUSIVE SALES AGENT: MEL BAY PUBLICATIONS, INC., PACIFIC, MO 63069. B.M.I. MADE AND PRINTED IN U.S.A.

Visit us on the Web at www.melbay.com — E-mail us at email@melbay.com

Table of Contents

About the book

Beyond Stick Control is the book that offers the snare and drumset player various eight bar solo studies to develop hand technique and hand/foot coordination. The book is divided into four sections: Part A: Hand Technique Development Studies, Part B: Hand/Foot Development, Part C: Ostinato Foot Pattern Development, and Part D: Linear Jazz Studies.

The hand technique solos in Part A serve as the foundation for the subsequent sections B, C, and D. Through the use of accents, single and double strokes, paradiddles, paradiddle-diddles, swiss army triplets and their respective inversions (sticking displacement), the beginning to advanced drummer will greatly improve hand technique, stick control and feel for the instrument.

Acknowledgements

I would like to thank all of the people who have given their support to my writing this snare/drumset book. Special thanks go to my loving wife Adriana, who assisted me in editing the text of the manuscript. Recognition is extended to my brother Gary and my parents, Isabel and Walter for their lifelong motivation.

The cover design is based upon a cherished painting by Luba Oleksiuk. Layout and publication design were accomplished by Dawn Hutchinson, with great appreciation.

Sincere gratitude go to Joe Holliday and the late Ted Reed for all their support and much-needed advice.

I would also like to thank Morris Lang, Roland Kohloff and Elden "Buster" Bailey for their expert snare drum instruction.

Finally, acknowledgement goes to Greg Dollmont, the staff, and students at Seminole Music.

Written/Edited by
Glenn W. Meyer

Editorial Assistant
Adriana Meyer

Music Layout/Publication Design
Dawn Hutchinson

Cover Design
Luba Oleksiuk

Rudiment Glossary for *Beyond Stick Control*

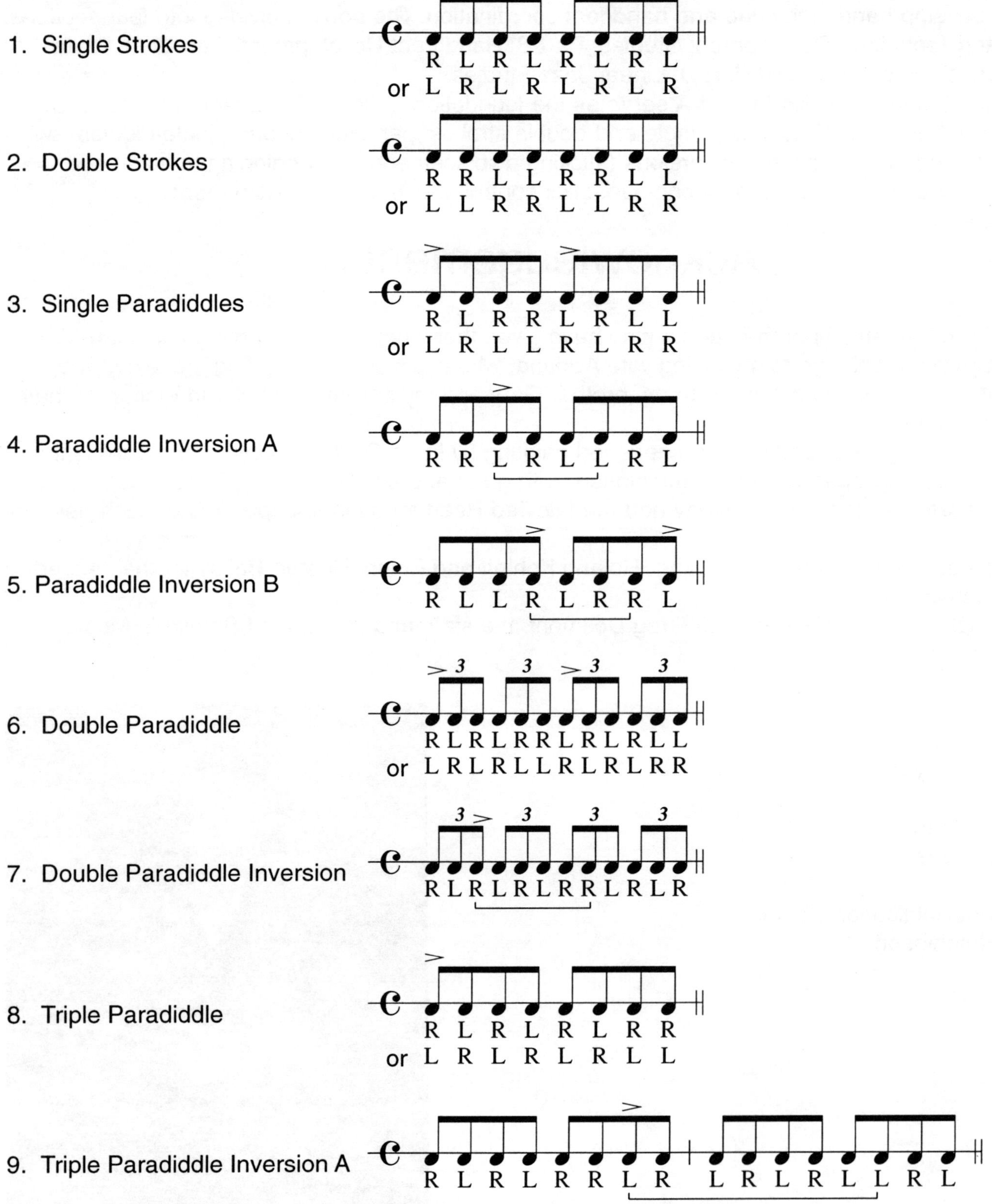

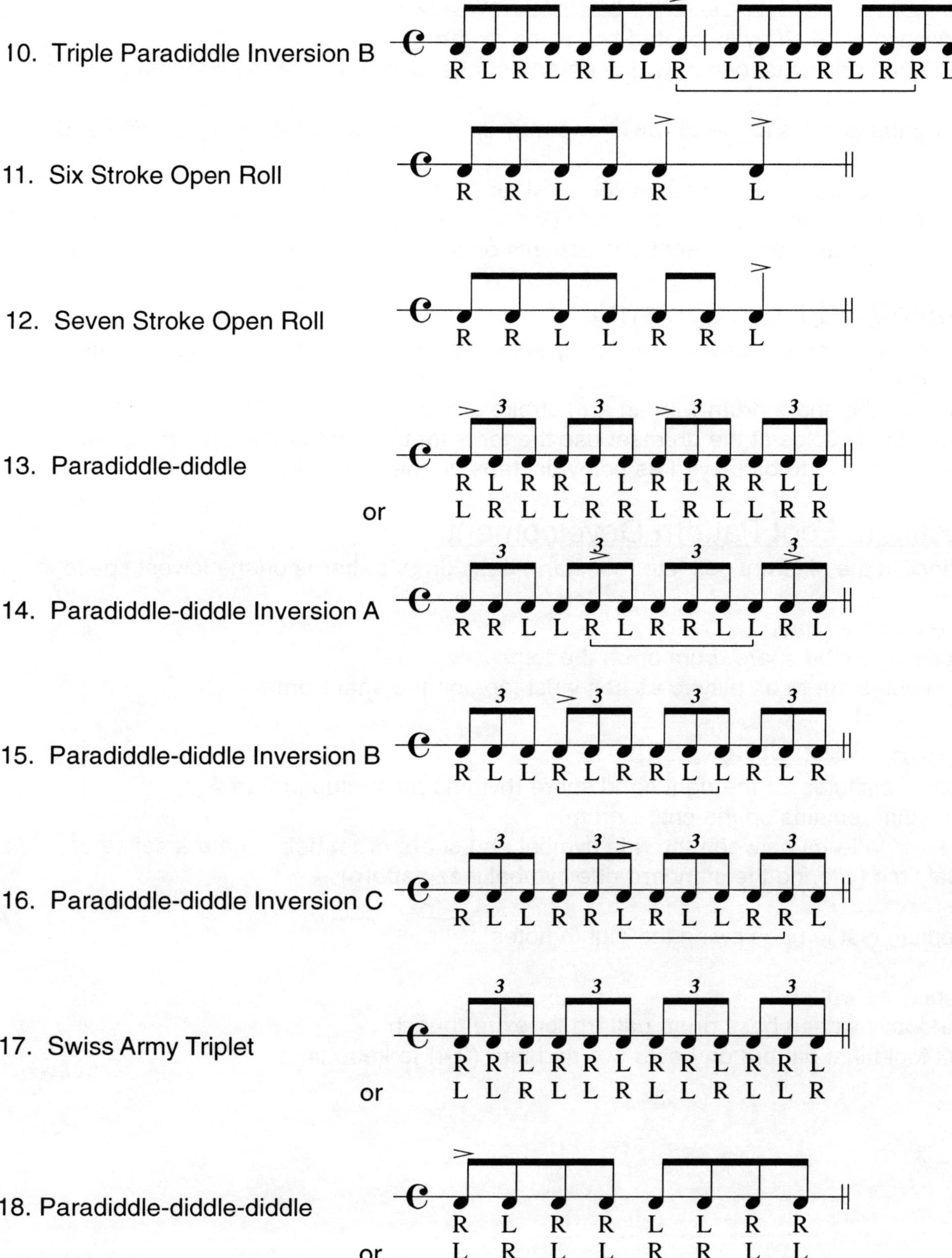
10. Triple Paradiddle Inversion B
R L R L R L L R L R L R L R R L
11. Six Stroke Open Roll
R R L L R L
12. Seven Stroke Open Roll
R R L L R R L
13. Paradiddle-diddle
3 3 3 3
R L R R L L R L R R L L
or
L R L L R R L R L L R R
14. Paradiddle-diddle Inversion A
3 3 3 3
R R L L R L R R L L R L
15. Paradiddle-diddle Inversion B
3 3 3 3
R L L R L R R L L R L R
16. Paradiddle-diddle Inversion C
3 3 3 3
R L L R R L R L L R R L
17. Swiss Army Triplet
3 3 3 3
R R L R R L R R L R R L
or
L L R L L R L L R L L R
18. Paradiddle-diddle-diddle
R L R R L L R R
or
L R L L R R L L

Performance Instructions for Beyond Stick Control

Part A Hand Technique Development Studies

- The sticking for each hand study is located below the rhythm.
- For right and left hand accents, one may use an arm stroke or rimshot when performing on the snare drum.
- When performing these solos at the drumset one may use the toms for the right and left hand accents.
- The unaccented notes are to be played as soft wrist taps on the snare drum.
- After mastering the above approaches, one may perform the right hand accents on the right crash cymbal with the bass drum, and the left hand accents on the left crash cymbal with the bass drum.

Part B Hand/Foot Development

- For these solo studies the bass drum is randomly substituting for some of the hand rhythms derived from Part A.
- Play the accents on the snare drum with an arm stroke or rim shot.
- When performing these solos at the drumset use the toms for the right and left hand accents.
- The unaccented notes are to be played as soft wrist taps on the snare drum.

Part C Ostinato Foot Pattern Development

- Feel free to pencil in the different ostinato (constant) bass drum patterns on the lowest space in the staff, one at a time.
- Keep strict time with the hihat.
- Perform the accents on the snare drum or on the toms.
- The unaccented notes are to be played as soft wrist taps on the snare drum.

Part D Linear Jazz Style

- The ride cymbal substitutes for the right hand snare rhythms presented in Part A.
- The left hand rhythm remains on the snare drum.
- The mixed sticking patterns between the ride cymbal and snare drum help create a sense of "broken" cymbal time (altering the standard ride cymbal jazz pattern).
- For slow to medium fast tempos swing the eighth notes = 3 .
- For uptempos play as written.
- Perform the randomly written bass drum pattern for extra "punch".
- Perform the left foot hihat pattern on beats two and four (2,4) to keep time.

Part A: Hand Technique Development

8 Bar Solos Using 8th Note Rhythms

Single/Double Stroke Study

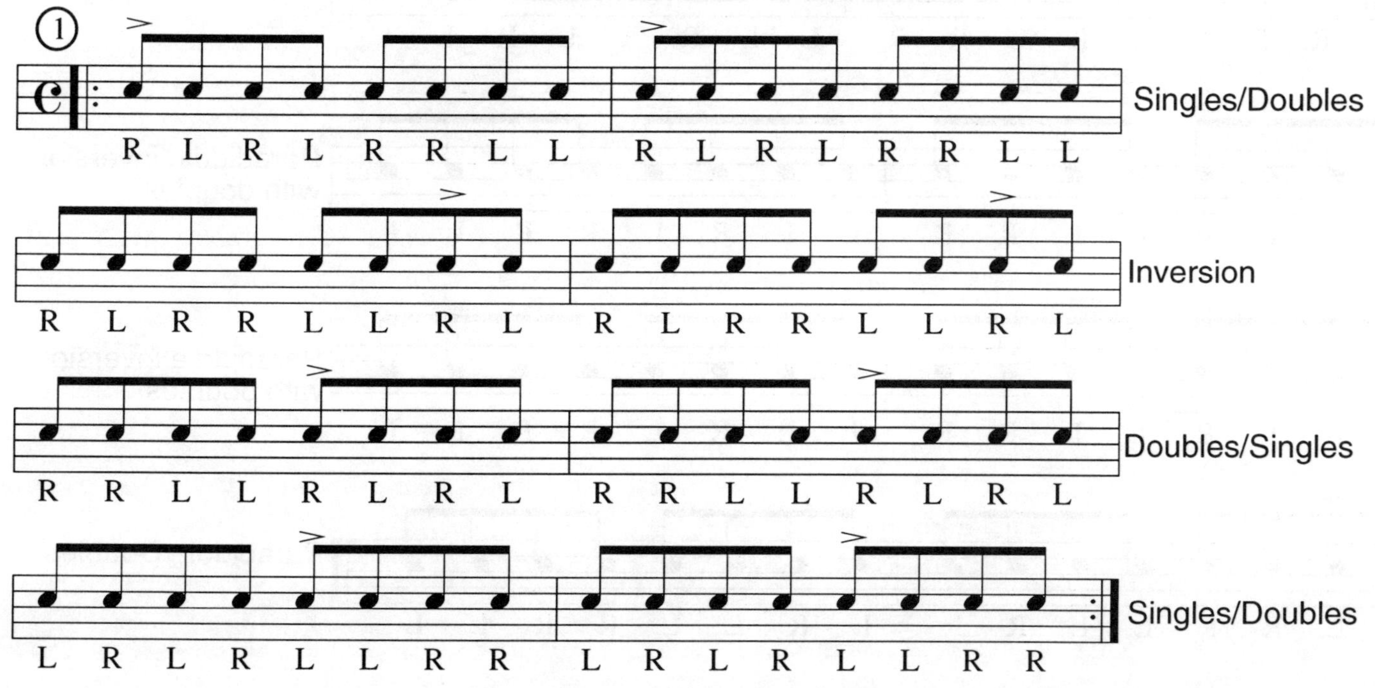

Part B: Hand/Foot Development

* All the 8 bar solos in Part B are derived from the Hand Technique Development Solos in Part A.

* The bass drum voicing randomly substitutes for some of the snare notes presented in Part A.

Doubles and Paradiddle Study

Part A

Part B

Six Stroke and Inversion Study

Part A

Part B

7 Stroke/Inversion Study

Part A

Part B

Paradiddle/Inversion Study

Part A

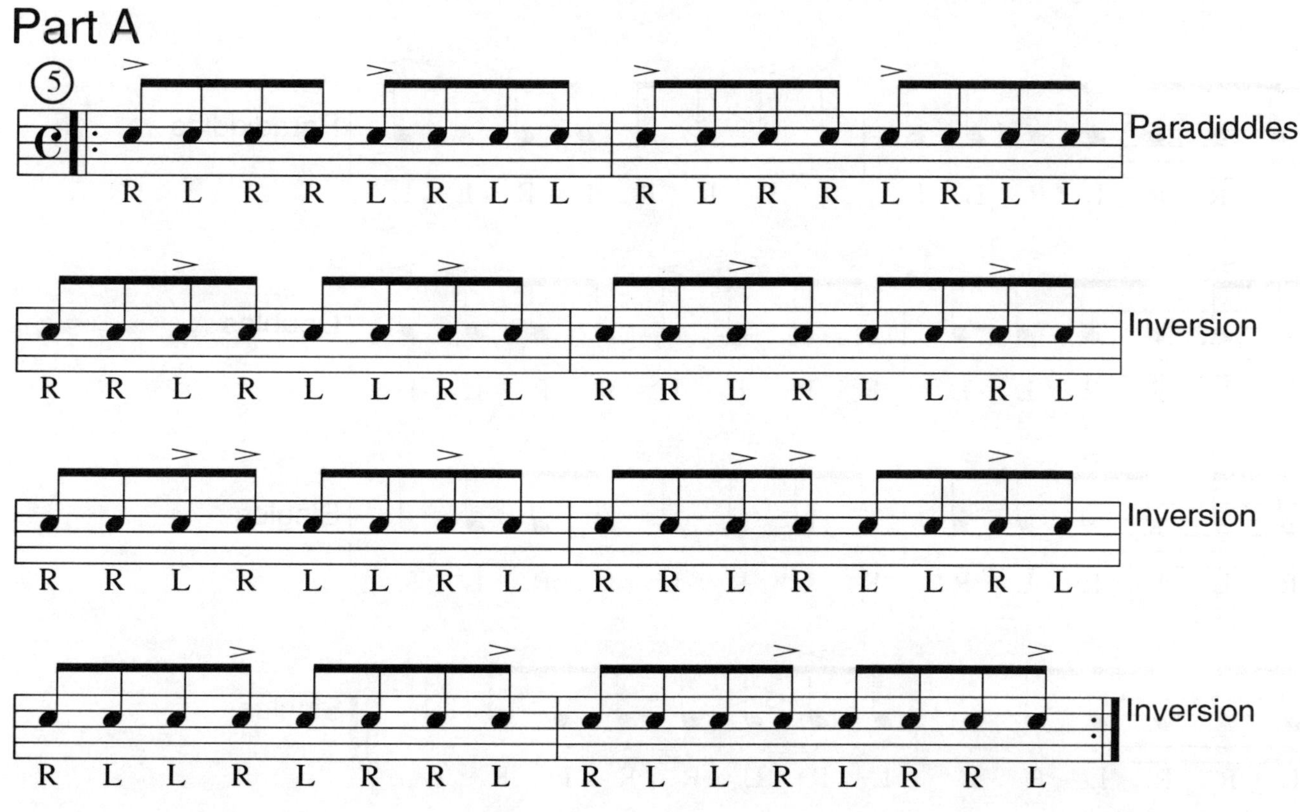

Part B

Paradiddle/Double/Single Stroke Study

Part A

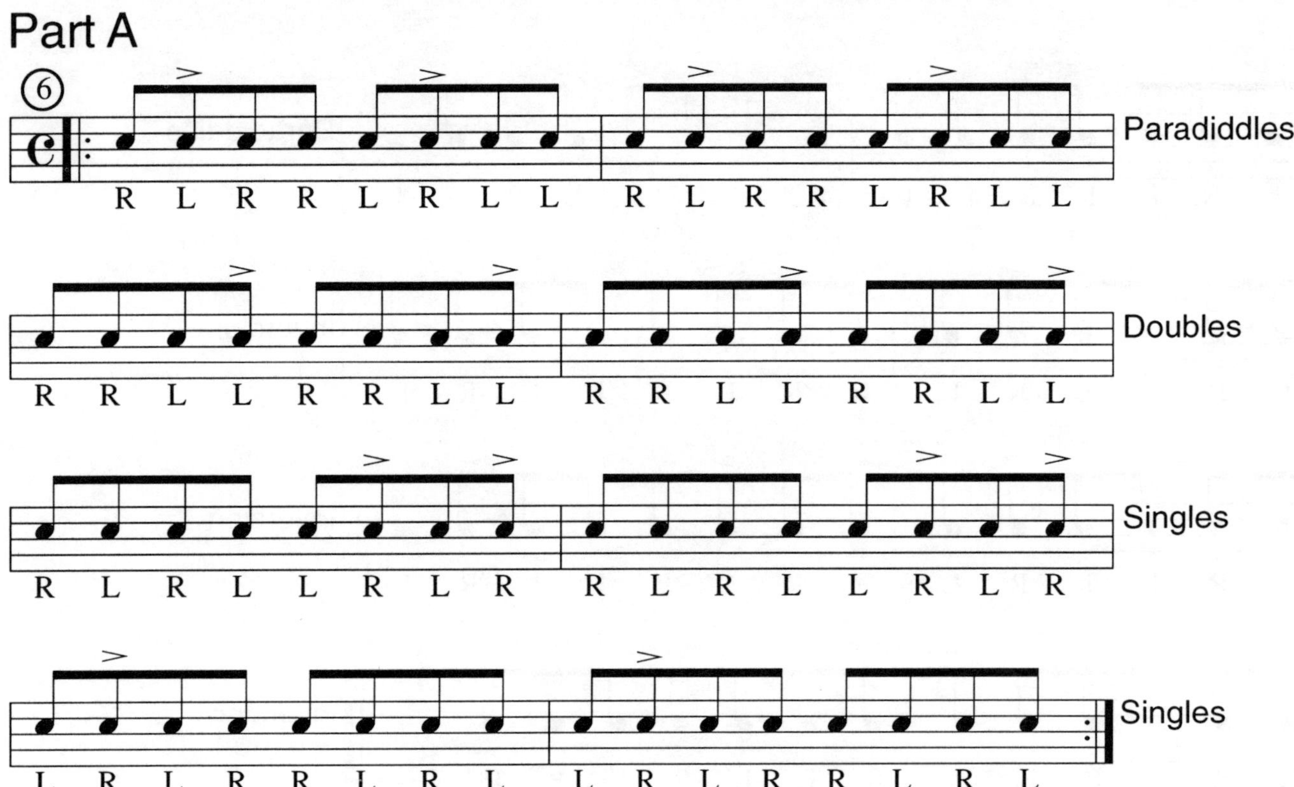

Part B

Doubles and Inverted Paradiddle Study

Part A

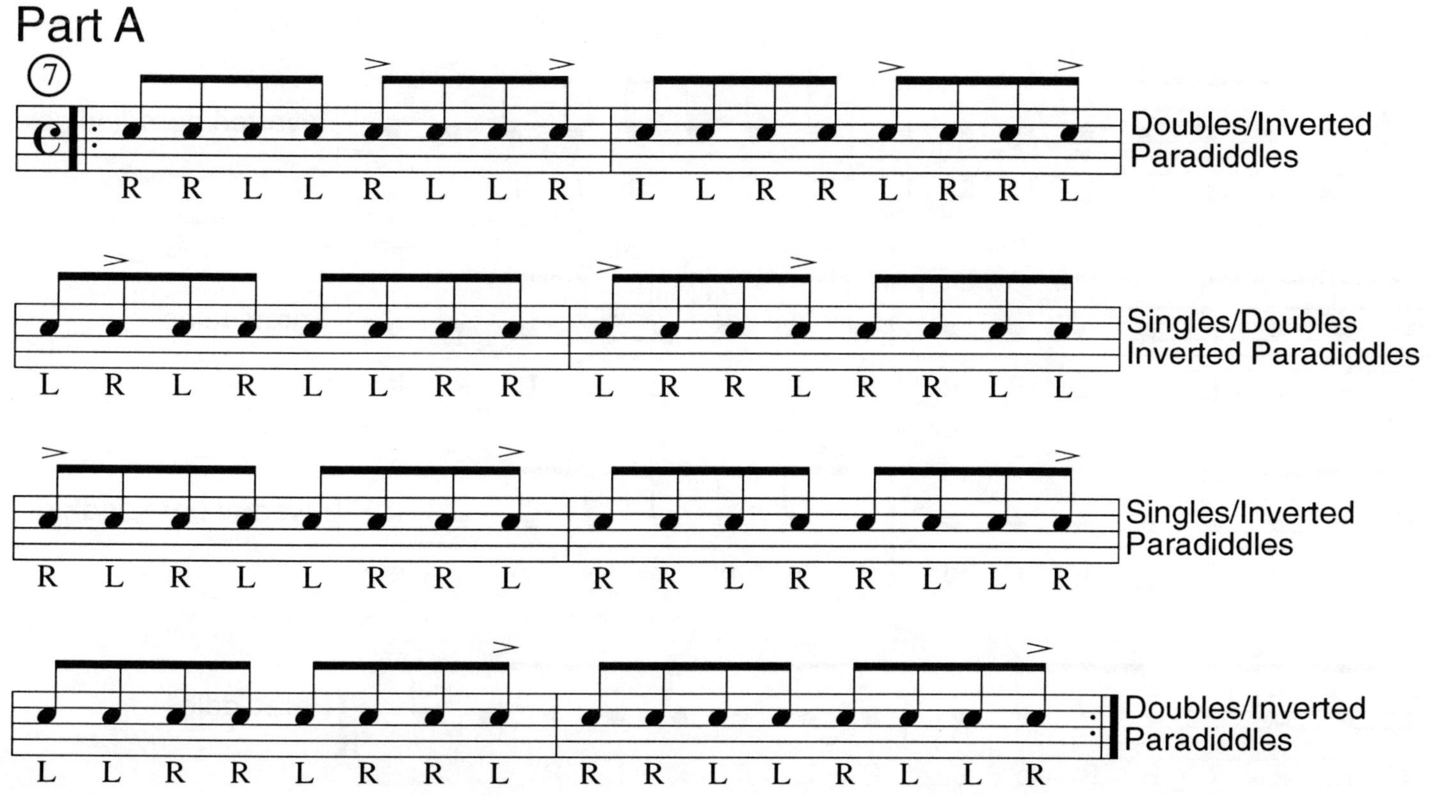

Part B

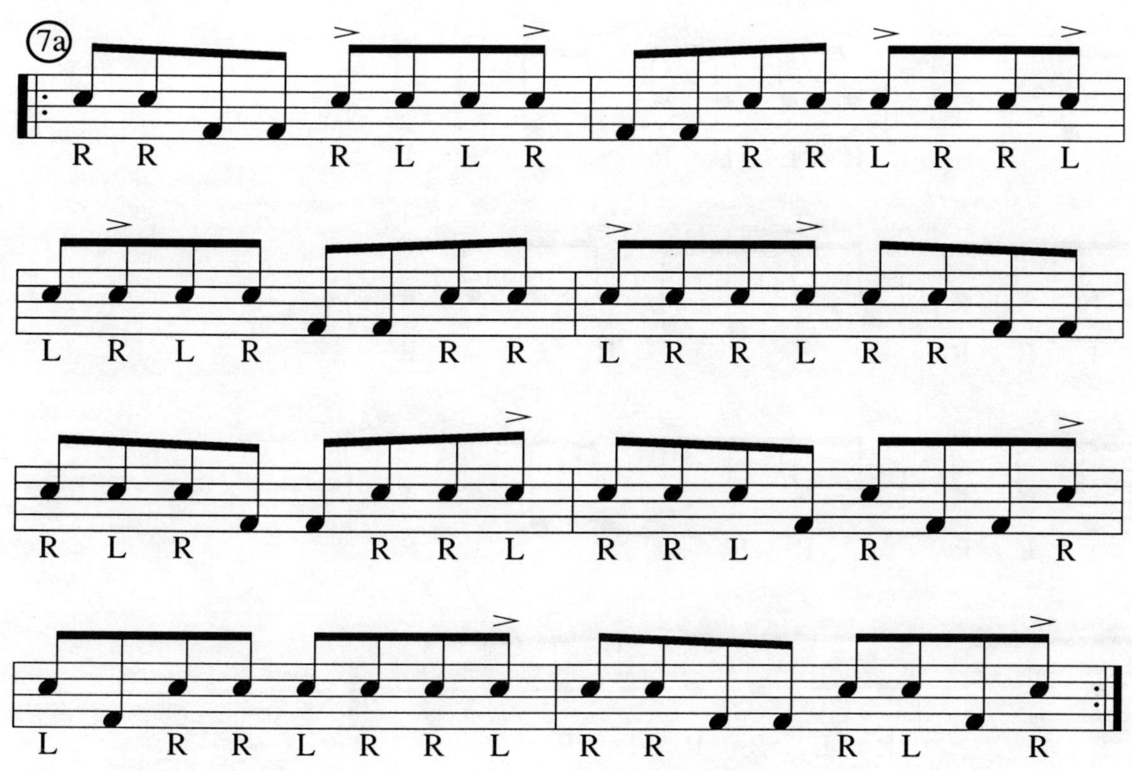

Inverted Paradiddle/Paradiddle Study

Part A

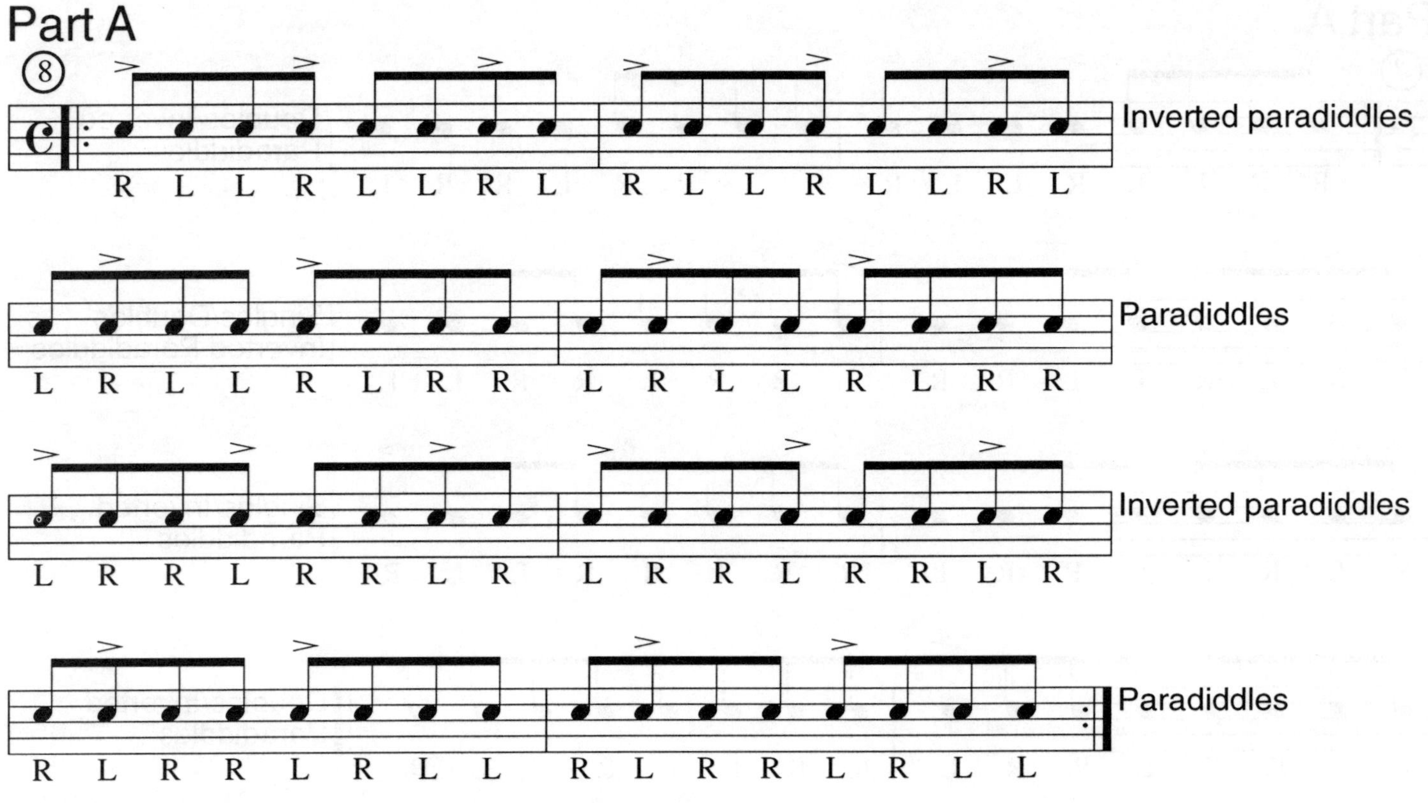

Part B

Paradiddle-diddle-diddle Study

Part A

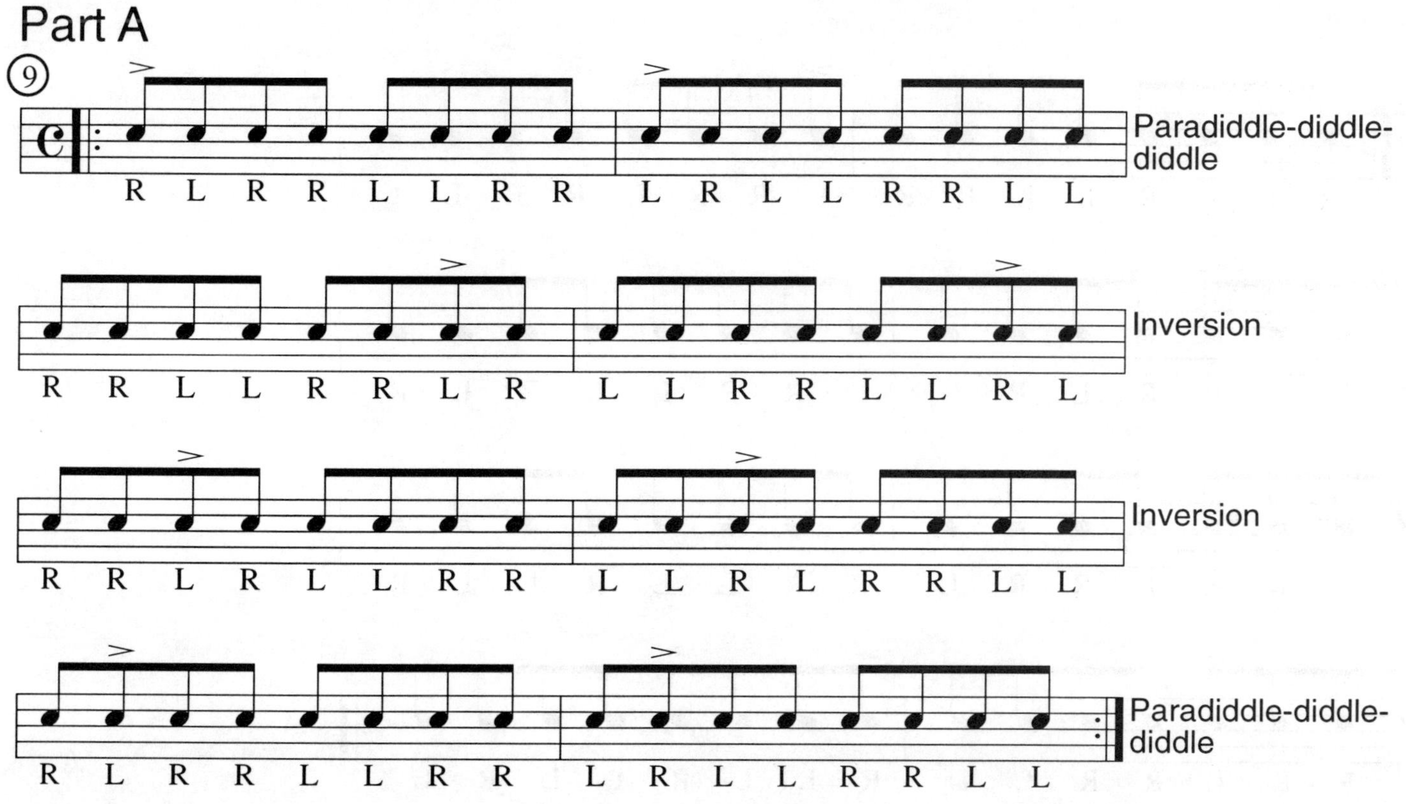

Part B

Mixed Sticking Study

Part A

Part B

Triple Paradiddle and Inversion Study

Part A

Part B

Inverted Paradiddles and Paradiddle Study

Part A

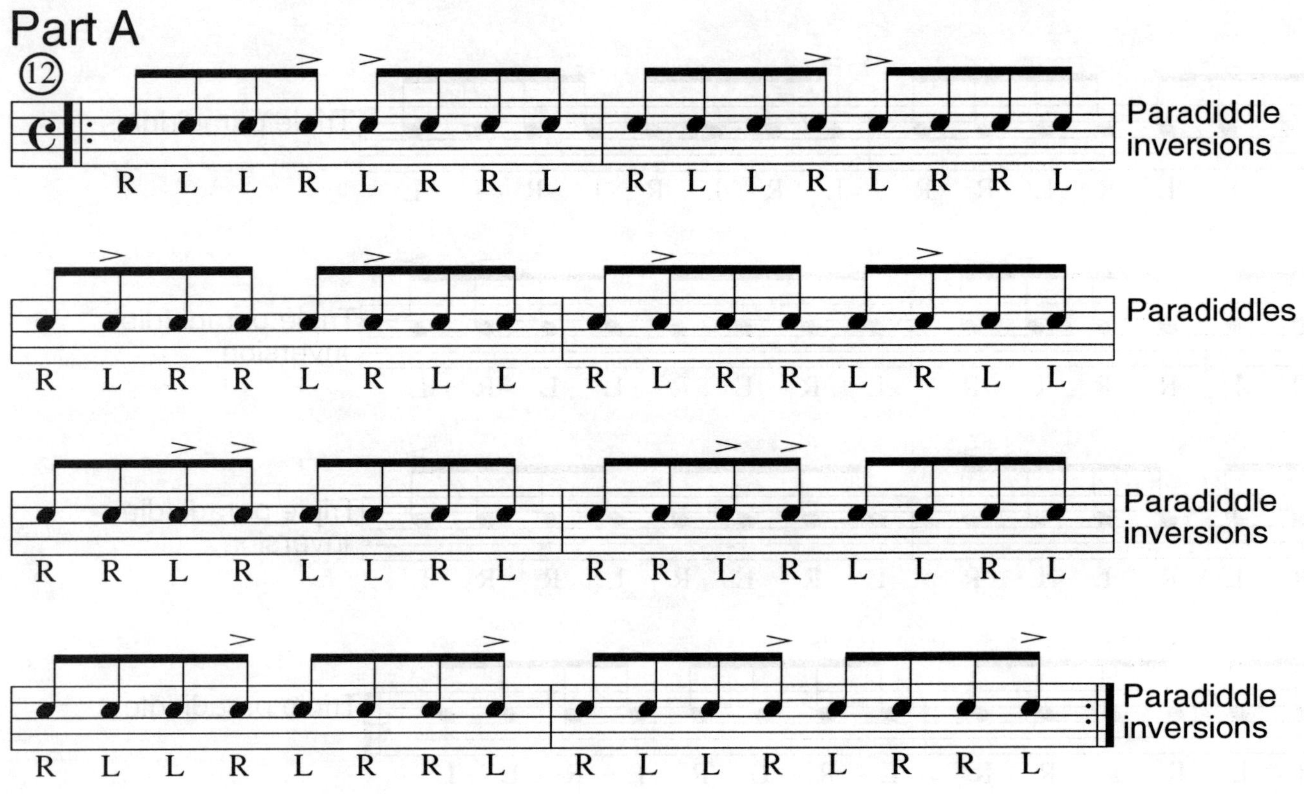

Part B

8 Bar Solos Using Triplet Rhythms

Single Stroke/Double Paradiddle Study

Part A

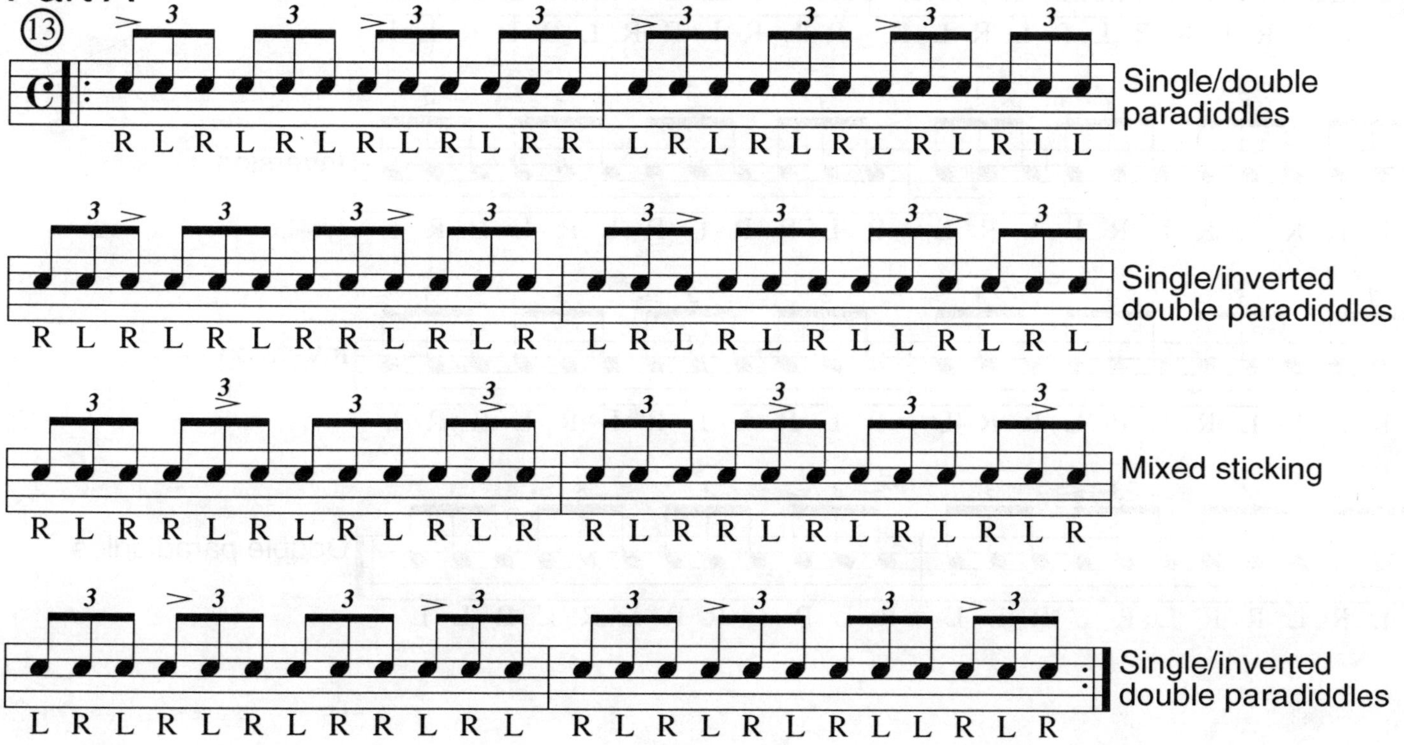
13
R L R L R L R L R L R R L R L R L R L R L R L L
Single/double paradiddles
R L R L R L R R L R L R L R L R L R L L R L R L
Single/inverted double paradiddles
R L R R L R L R L R L R R L R R L R L R L R L R
Mixed sticking
L R L R L R L R R L R L R L R L R L R L L R L R
Single/inverted double paradiddles

Part B

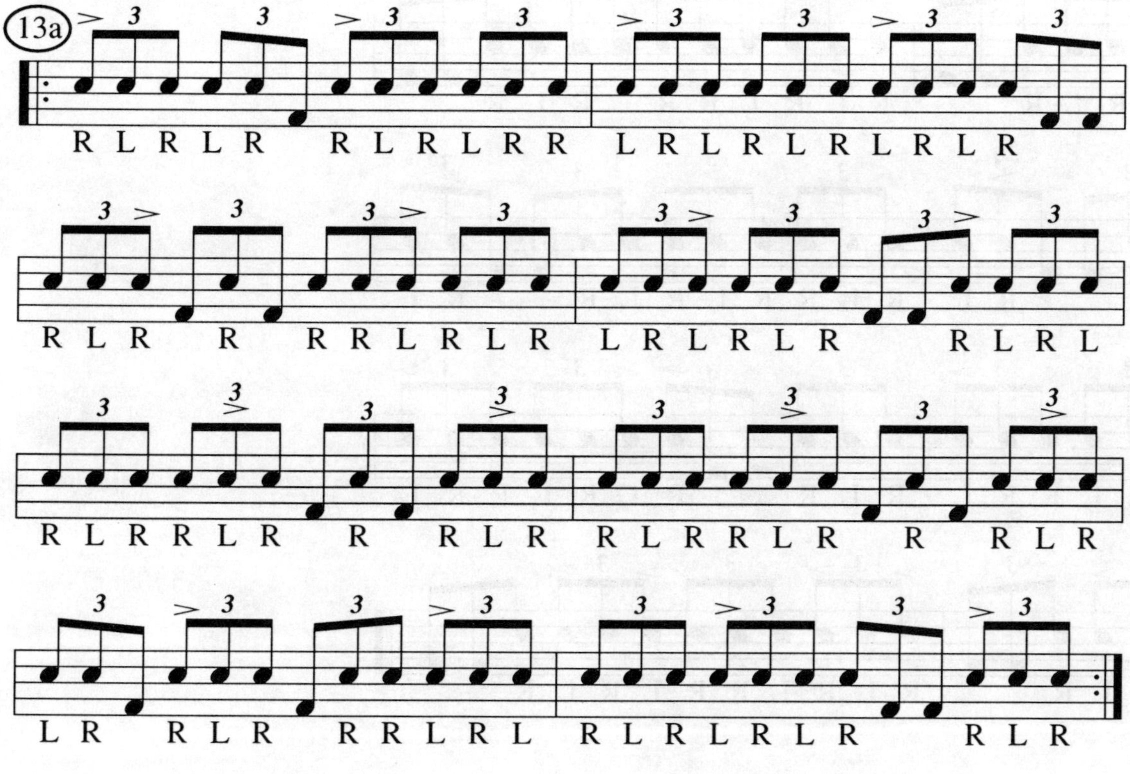
13a
R L R L R R L R L R R L R L R L R L R L R
R L R R R R L R L R L R L R L R R L R L
R L R R L R R R L R R L R R L R R R L R
L R R L R R R L R L R L R L R L R R L R

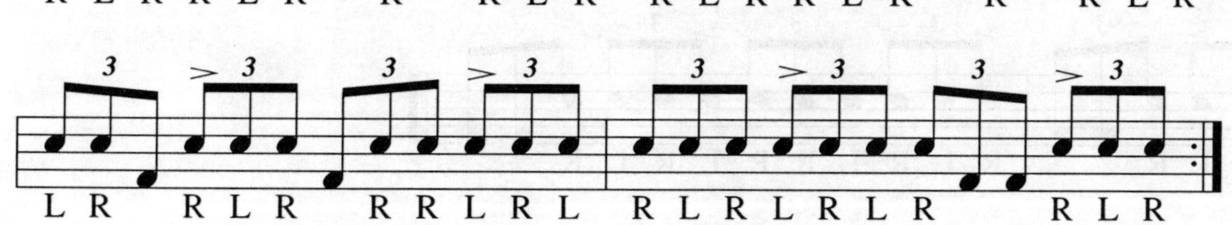

Double Paradiddle/Inversion Study

Part A

Part B

Paradiddle-diddle/Inversion Study

Part A

Part B

Mixed Sticking Study

Part A

Part B

Swiss Army Triplet/Mixed Sticking Study

Part A

Part B

Mixed Sticking Study

Part A

Part B

8 Bar Solos Using 8th Notes and Triplets

Mixed Sticking Study

Swiss Army and Single Stroke Study

Part A

Part B

8 Bar Solos Using 16th Note Rhythms

Singles

Part A

(21)

R L R L R L R L R L R L R L R L   R L R L R L R L R L R L R L R L
L R L R L R L R L R L R L R L R   L R L R L R L R L R L R L R L R

R L R L R L R L R L R L R L R L   R L R L R L R L R L R L R L R L
L R L R L R L R L R L R L R L R   L R L R L R L R L R L R L R L R

R L R L R L R L R L R L R L R L   R L R L R L R L R L R L R L R L
L R L R L R L R L R L R L R L R   L R L R L R L R L R L R L R L R

R L R L R L R L R L R L R L R L   R L R L R L R L R L R L R L R L
L R L R L R L R L R L R L R L R   L R L R L R L R L R L R L R L R

Part B

(21a)

R L R L R L R   R L R L R   R L   R L R   R L R L R L R L R L R
L R L R L R L   L R L R L   L R   L R L   L R L R L R L R L R L

R L R L   R L R L R L   R L   R L R L R L   L R L R L R L   L
L R L R   L R L R L R   L R   L R L R L R   R L R L R L R   R

R L R L R L   R L R L R L   R L R L R L R L   L R   L R
L R L R L R   L R L R L R   L R L R L R L R   R L   R L

R L R L   R L R L R L   R L   R L R L R   R L R L R L R   R L
L R L R   L R L R L R   L R   L R L R L   L R L R L R L   L R

Mixed Sticking Study

Part A

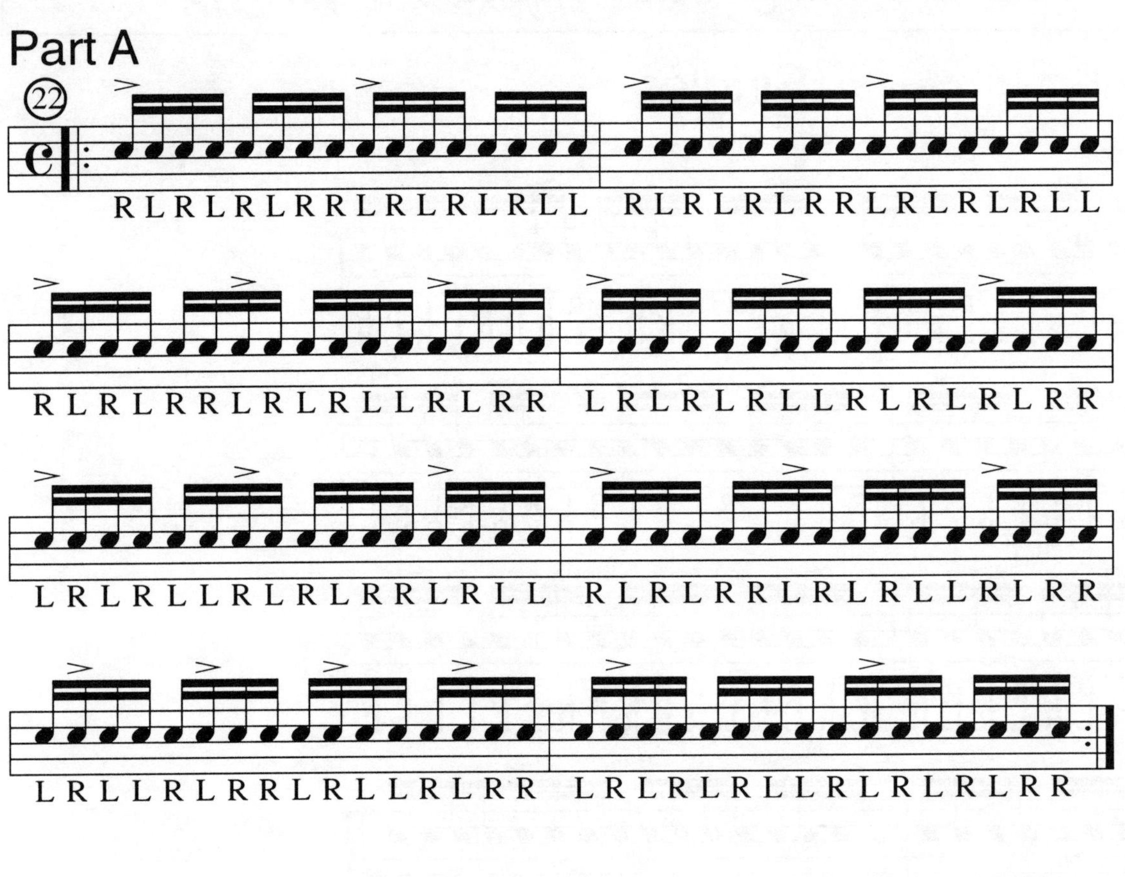

Part B

16th Note Accent Study

Phrasing in 3/16, 5/16, 7/16, and 3/16 Meter

Part A

Part B

Ostinato Foot Pattern Development

8 Bar Solos Using 8th Note Rhythms

For Part C, choose and play one bass drum and hihat foot pattern for the 8 bar hand solo. See bottom of page for further instructions.

Part C

Single/Double Stroke Study

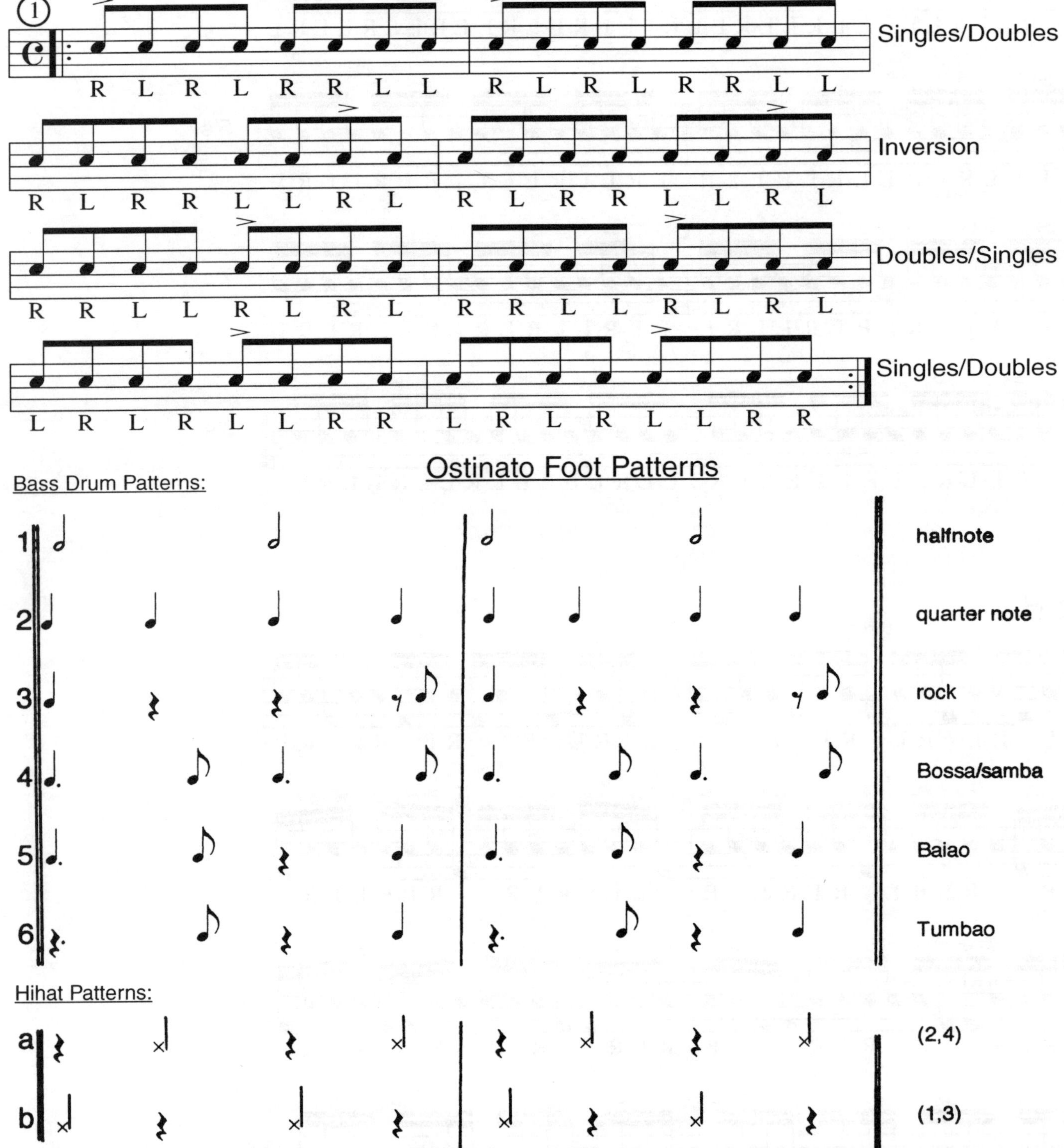

- Feel free to pencil in the different ostinato (constant) bass drum patterns on the lowest space in the staff, for the 8 bar hand solo located above.
- One may also choose and pencil in a desired hihat foot pattern.

Doubles and Paradiddle Study

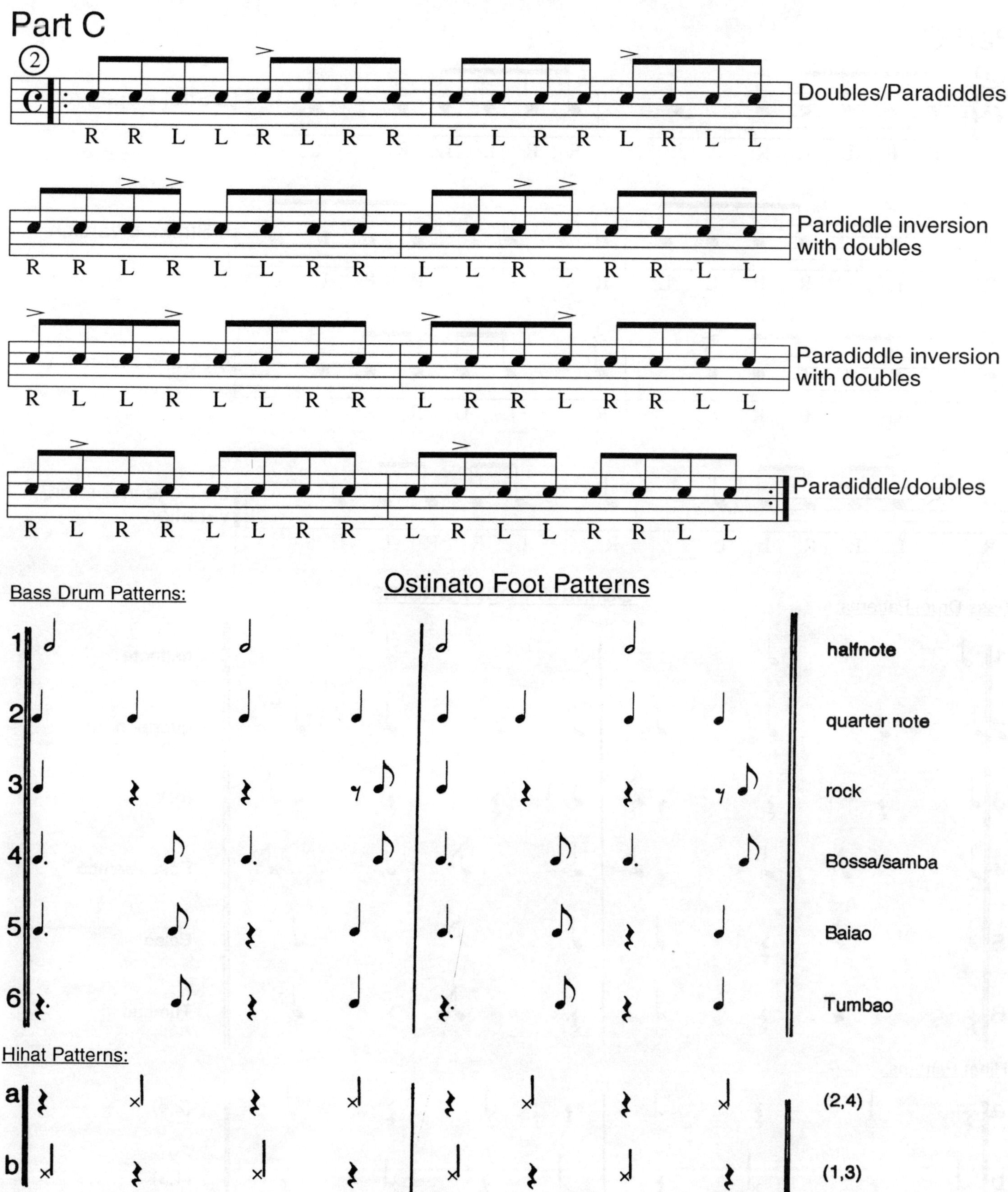

- Feel free to pencil in the different ostinato (constant) bass drum patterns on the lowest space in the staff, for the 8 bar hand solo located above.
- One may also choose and pencil in a desired hihat foot pattern.

Six Stroke and Inversion Study

- Feel free to pencil in the different ostinato (constant) bass drum patterns on the lowest space in the staff, for the 8 bar hand solo located above.
- One may also choose and pencil in a desired hihat foot pattern.

7 Stroke/Inversion Study

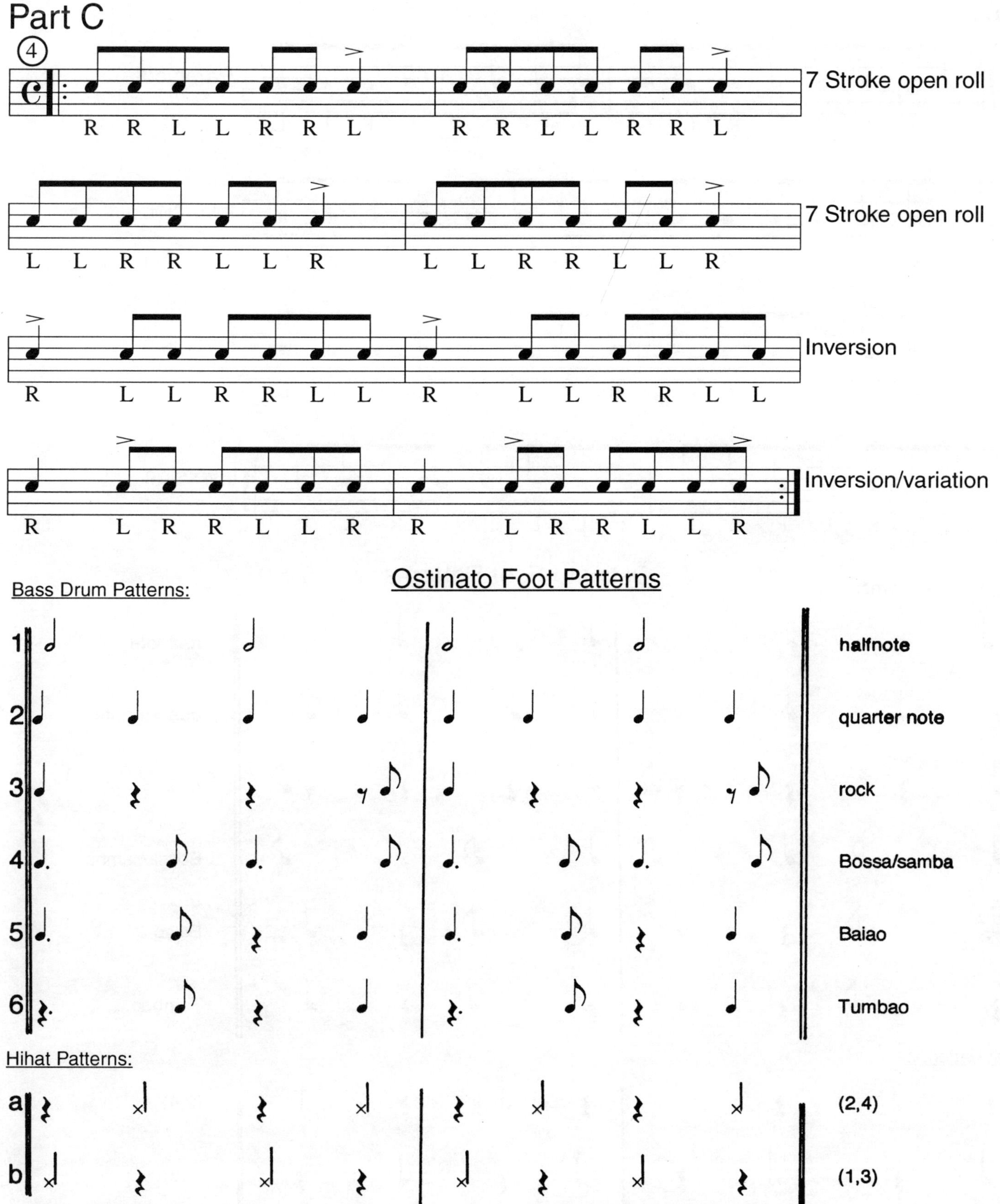

- Feel free to pencil in the different ostinato (constant) bass drum patterns on the lowest space in the staff, for the 8 bar hand solo located above.
- One may also choose and pencil in a desired hihat foot pattern.

Paradiddle/Inversion Study

Part C

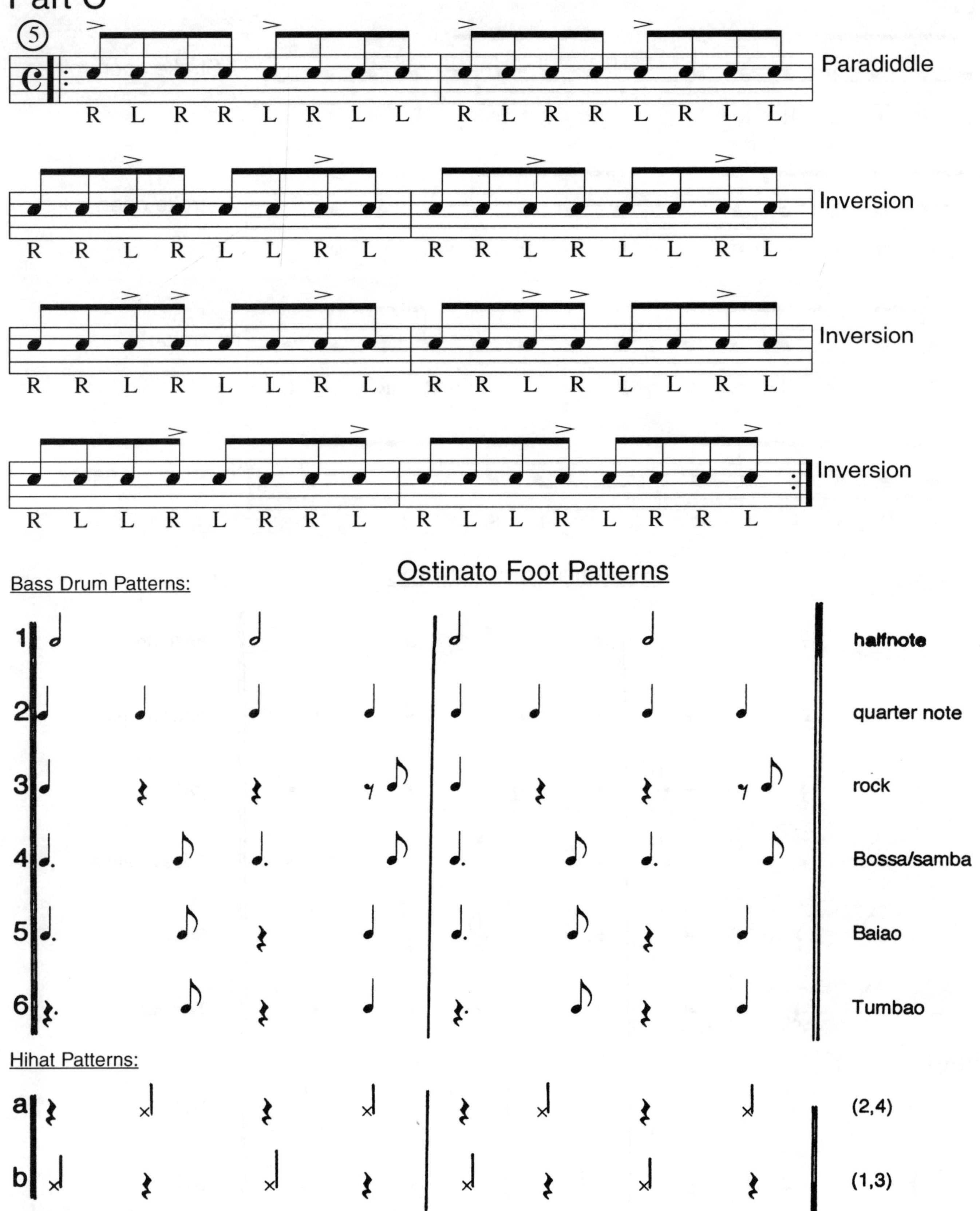

- Feel free to pencil in the different ostinato (constant) bass drum patterns on the lowest space in the staff, for the 8 bar hand solo located above.
- One may also choose and pencil in a desired hihat foot pattern.

Paradiddle/Double/Single Stroke Study

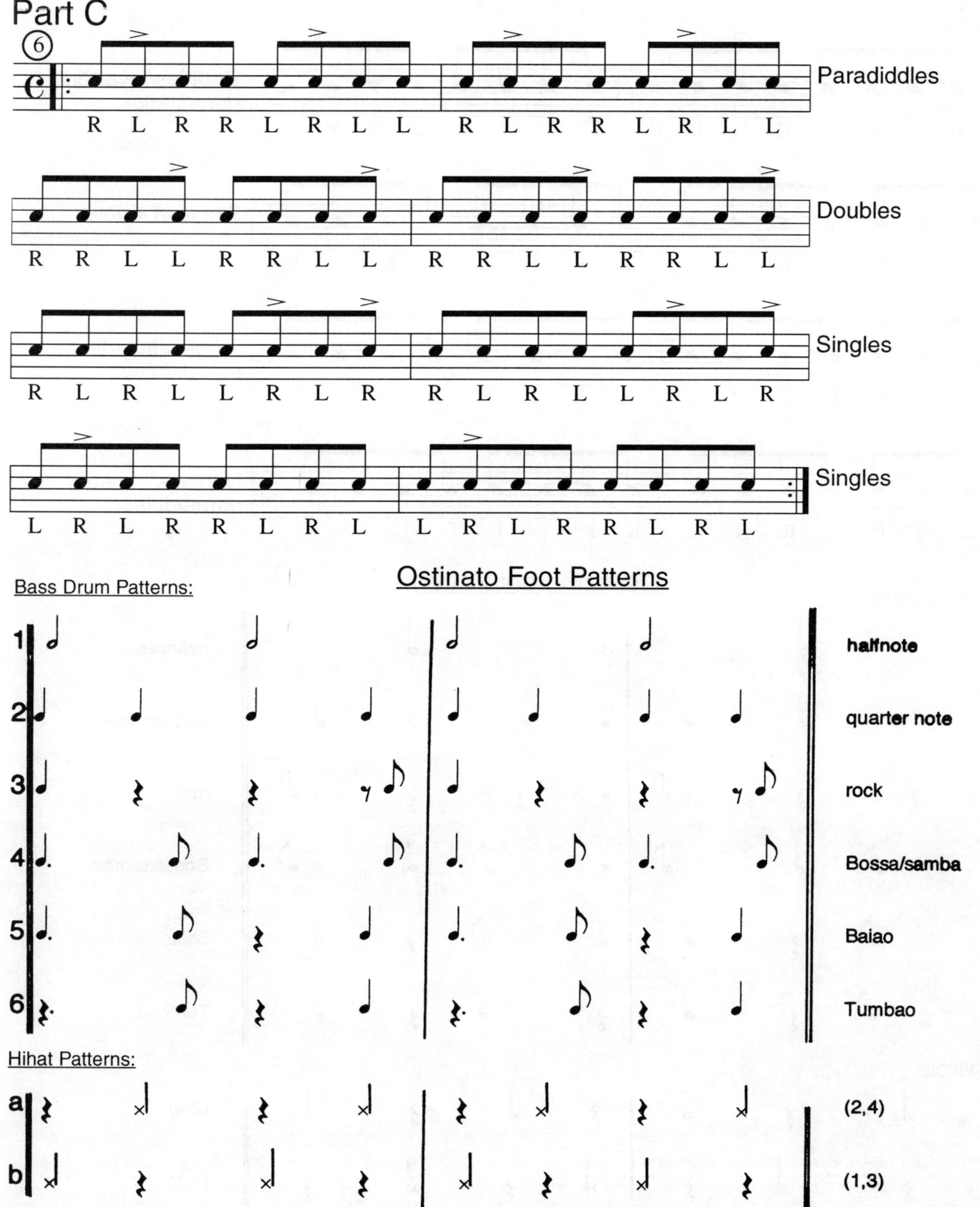

- Feel free to pencil in the different ostinato (constant) bass drum patterns on the lowest space in the staff, for the 8 bar hand solo located above.
- One may also choose and pencil in a desired hihat foot pattern.

Doubles and Inverted Paradiddle Study

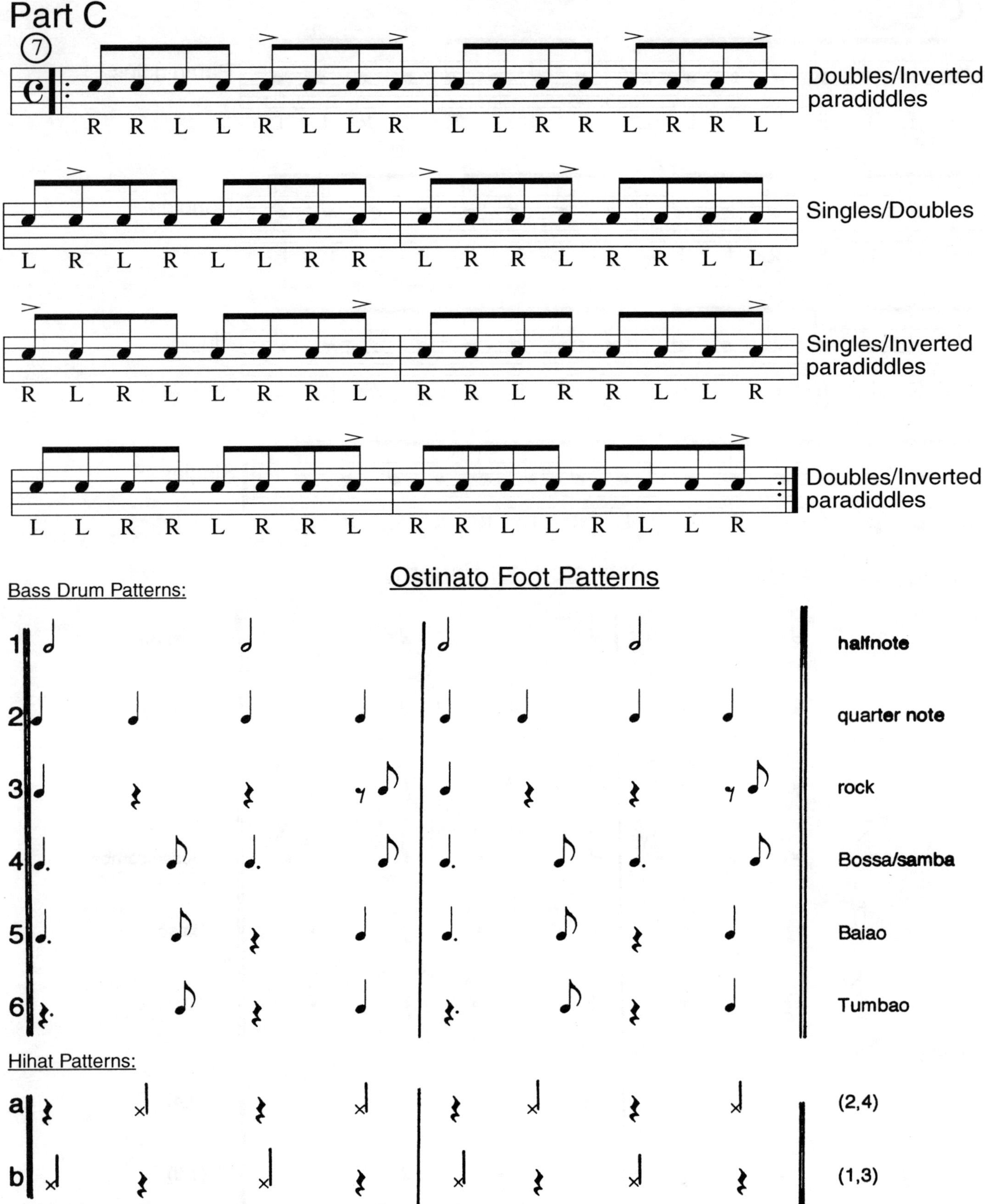

- Feel free to pencil in the different ostinato (constant) bass drum patterns on the lowest space in the staff, for the 8 bar hand solo located above.
- One may also choose and pencil in a desired hihat foot pattern.

Inverted Paradiddle/Paradiddle Study

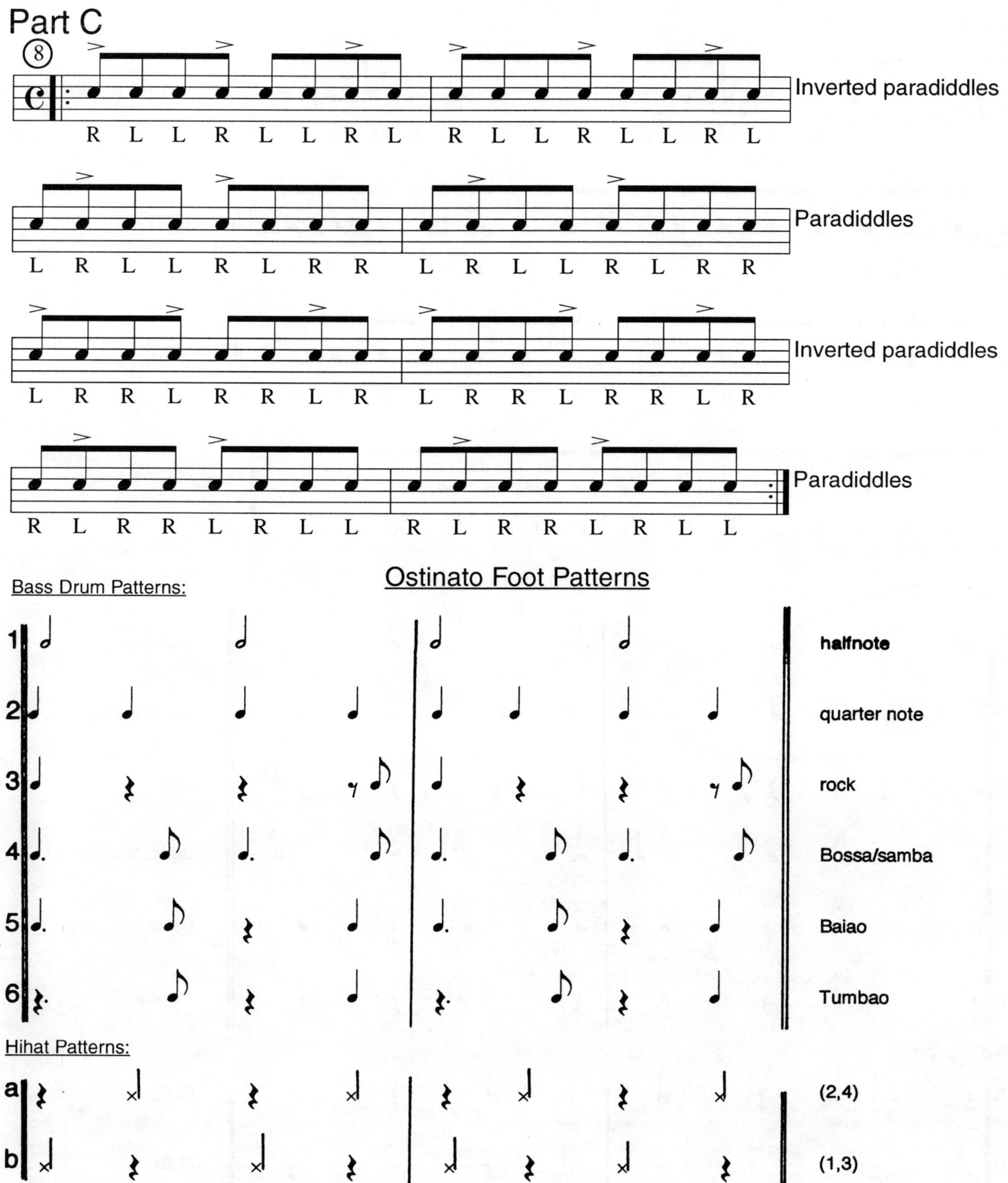

- Feel free to pencil in the different ostinato (constant) bass drum patterns on the lowest space in the staff, for the 8 bar hand solo located above.
- One may also choose and pencil in a desired hihat foot pattern.

Paradiddle-diddle-diddle Study

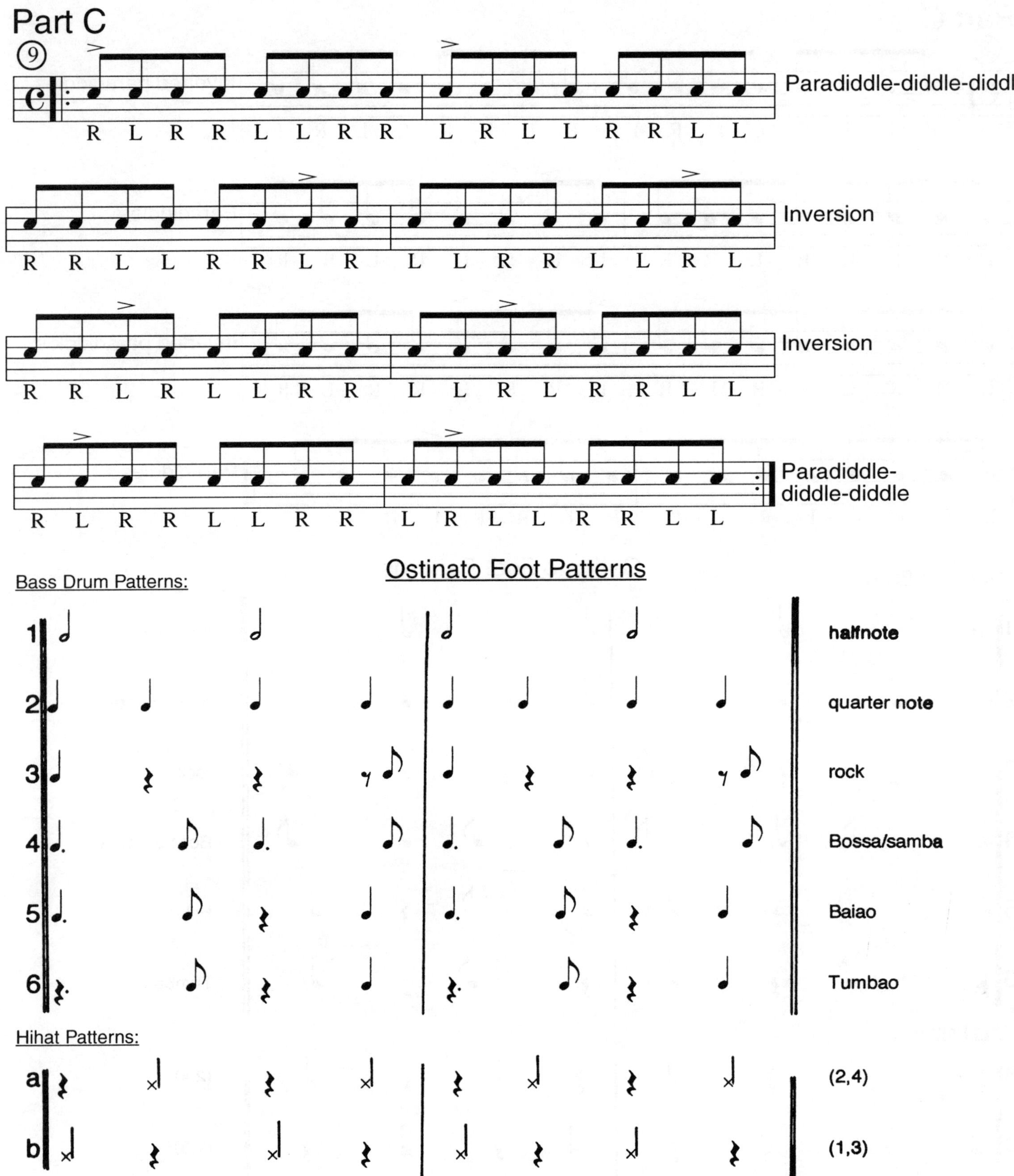

- Feel free to pencil in the different ostinato (constant) bass drum patterns on the lowest space in the staff, for the 8 bar hand solo located above.
- One may also choose and pencil in a desired hihat foot pattern.

Mixed Sticking Study

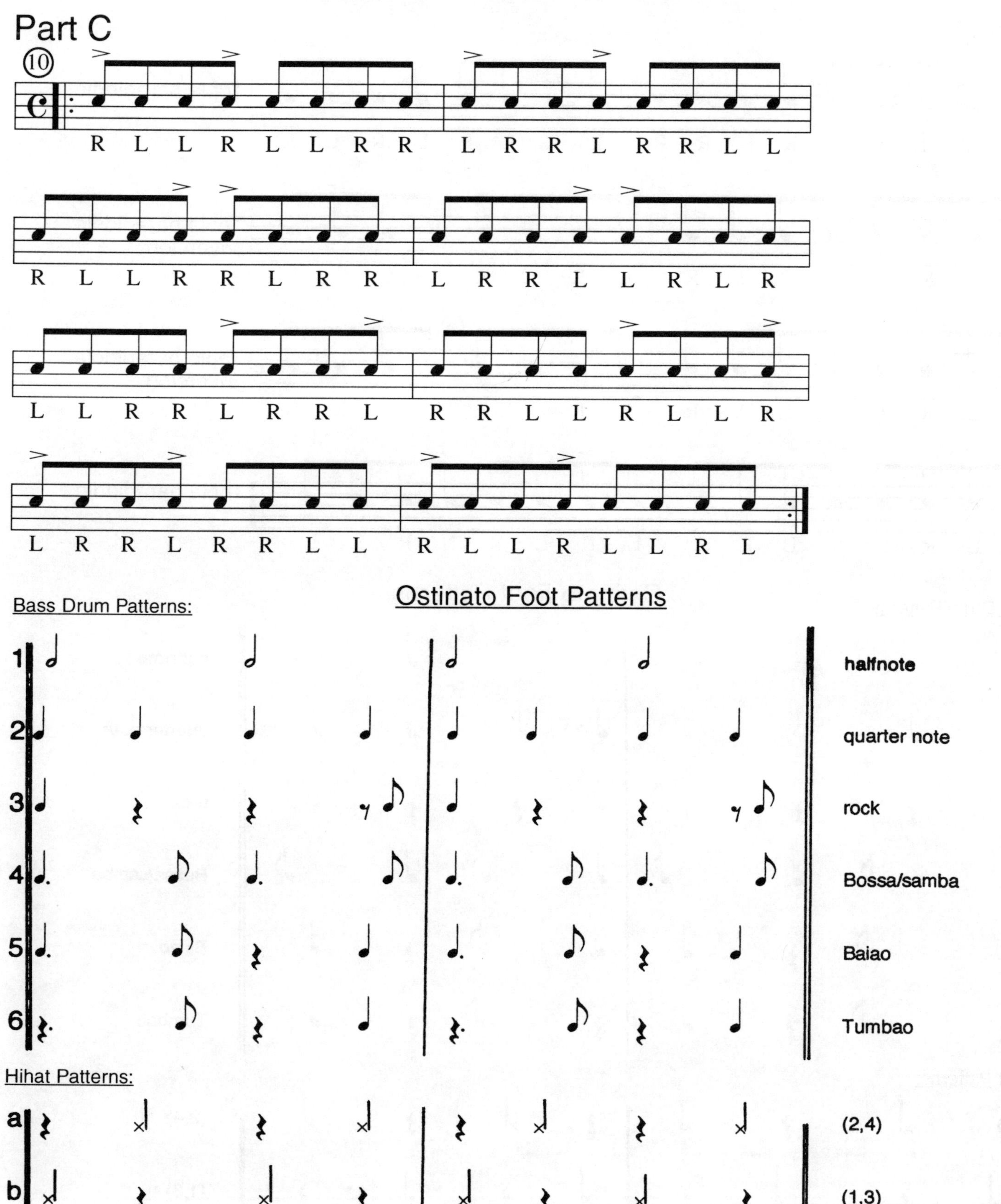

- Feel free to pencil in the different ostinato (constant) bass drum patterns on the lowest space in the staff, for the 8 bar hand solo located above.
- One may also choose and pencil in a desired hihat foot pattern.

Triple Paradiddle and Inversion Study

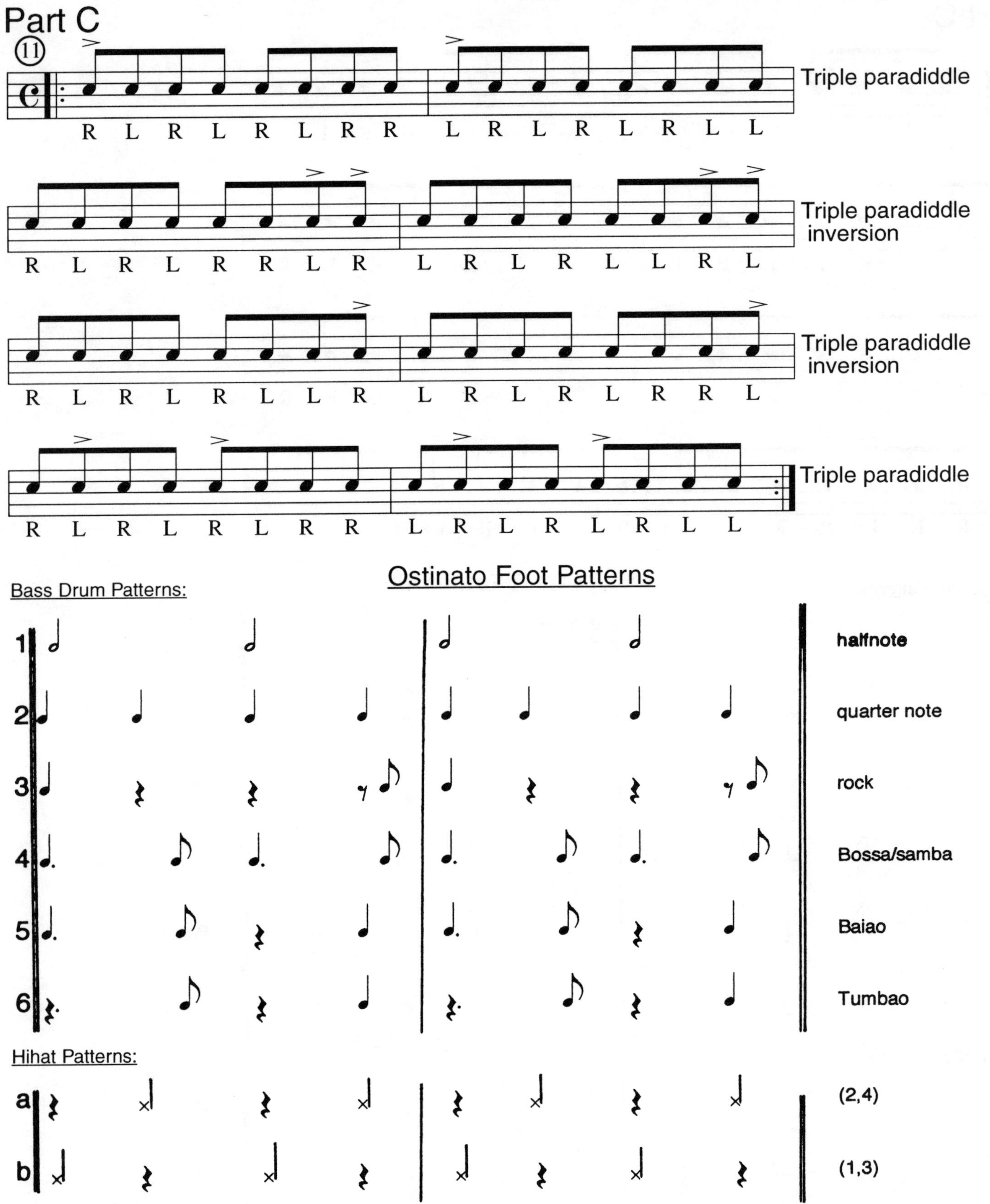

- Feel free to pencil in the different ostinato (constant) bass drum patterns on the lowest space in the staff, for the 8 bar hand solo located above.
- One may also choose and pencil in a desired hihat foot pattern.

Inverted Paradiddles and Paradiddle Study

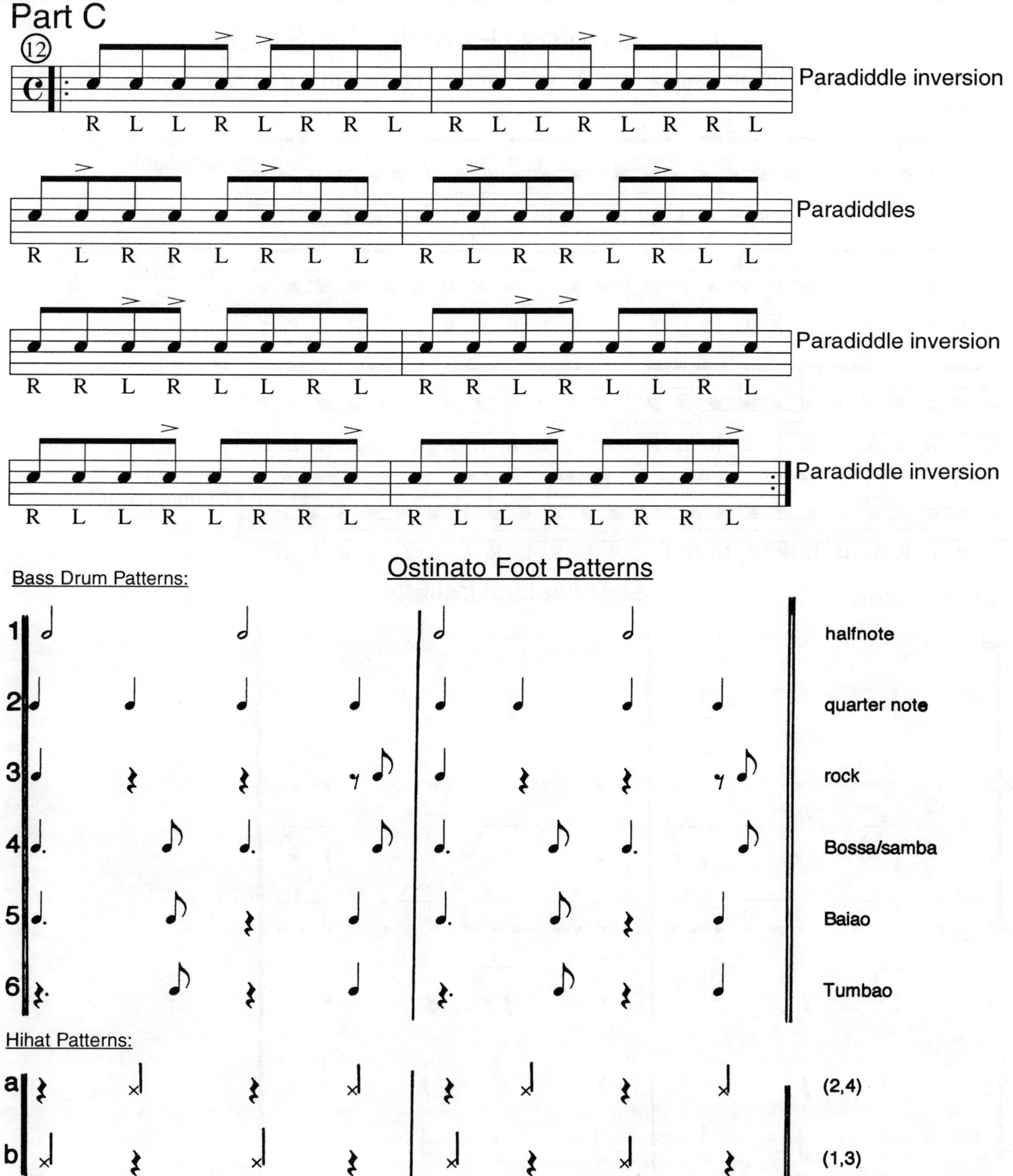

- Feel free to pencil in the different ostinato (constant) bass drum patterns on the lowest space in the staff, for the 8 bar hand solo located above.
- One may also choose and pencil in a desired hihat foot pattern.

8 Bar Solos Using Triplet Rhythms

Singles, Doubles, Paradiddle Study

Work through the new set of ostinato foot patterns located at the bottom of the page.

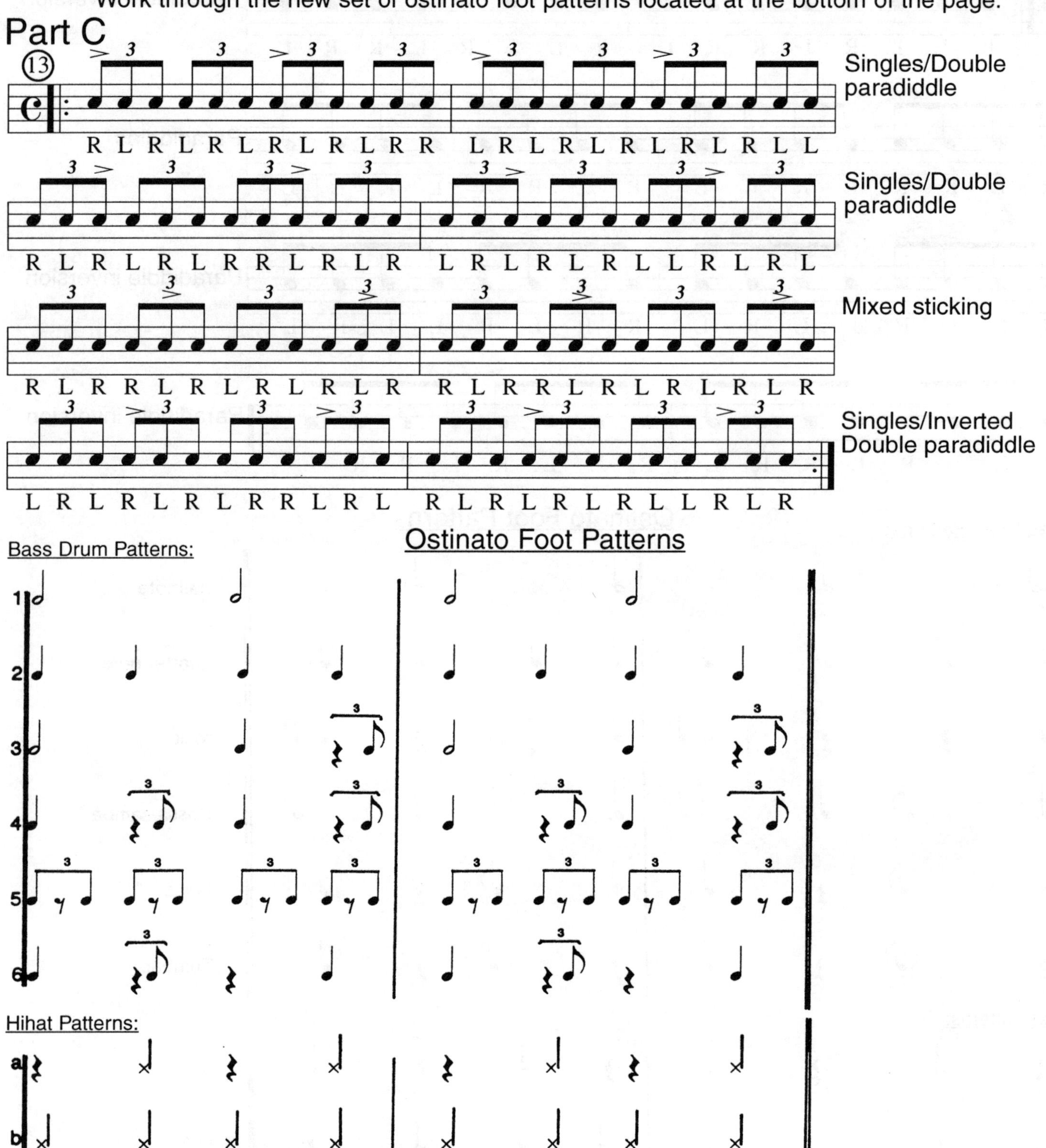

- Feel free to pencil in the different ostinato (constant) bass drum patterns on the lowest space in the staff, for the 8 bar hand solo located above.
- One may also choose and pencil in a desired hihat foot pattern.

Double Paradiddle/Inversion Study

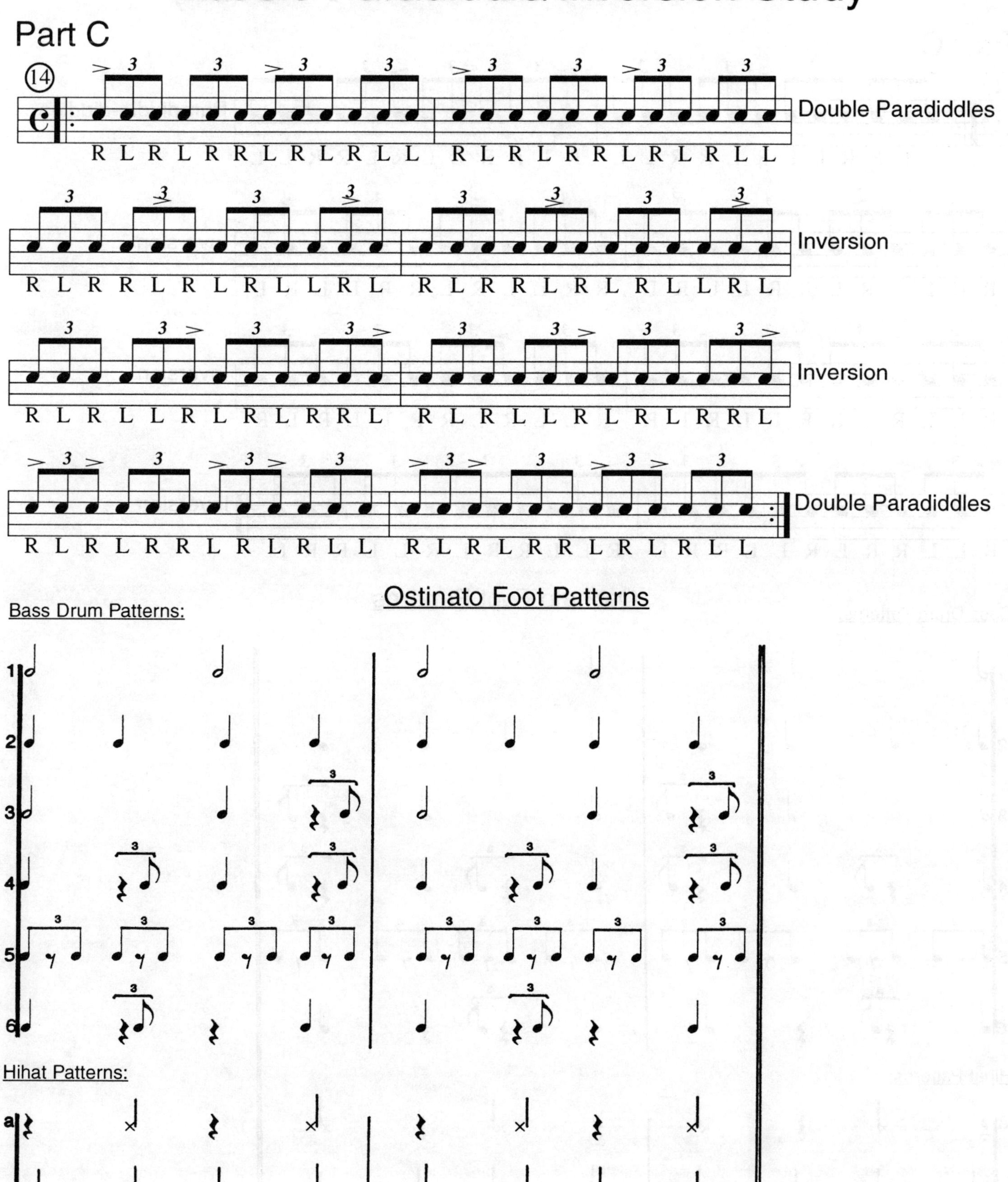

- Feel free to pencil in the different ostinato (constant) bass drum patterns on the lowest space in the staff, for the 8 bar hand solo located above.
- One may also choose and pencil in a desired hihat foot pattern.

Paradiddle-diddle/Inversion Study

- Feel free to pencil in the different ostinato (constant) bass drum patterns on the lowest space in the staff, for the 8 bar hand solo located above.
- One may also choose and pencil in a desired hihat foot pattern.

Mixed Sticking Study

Part C

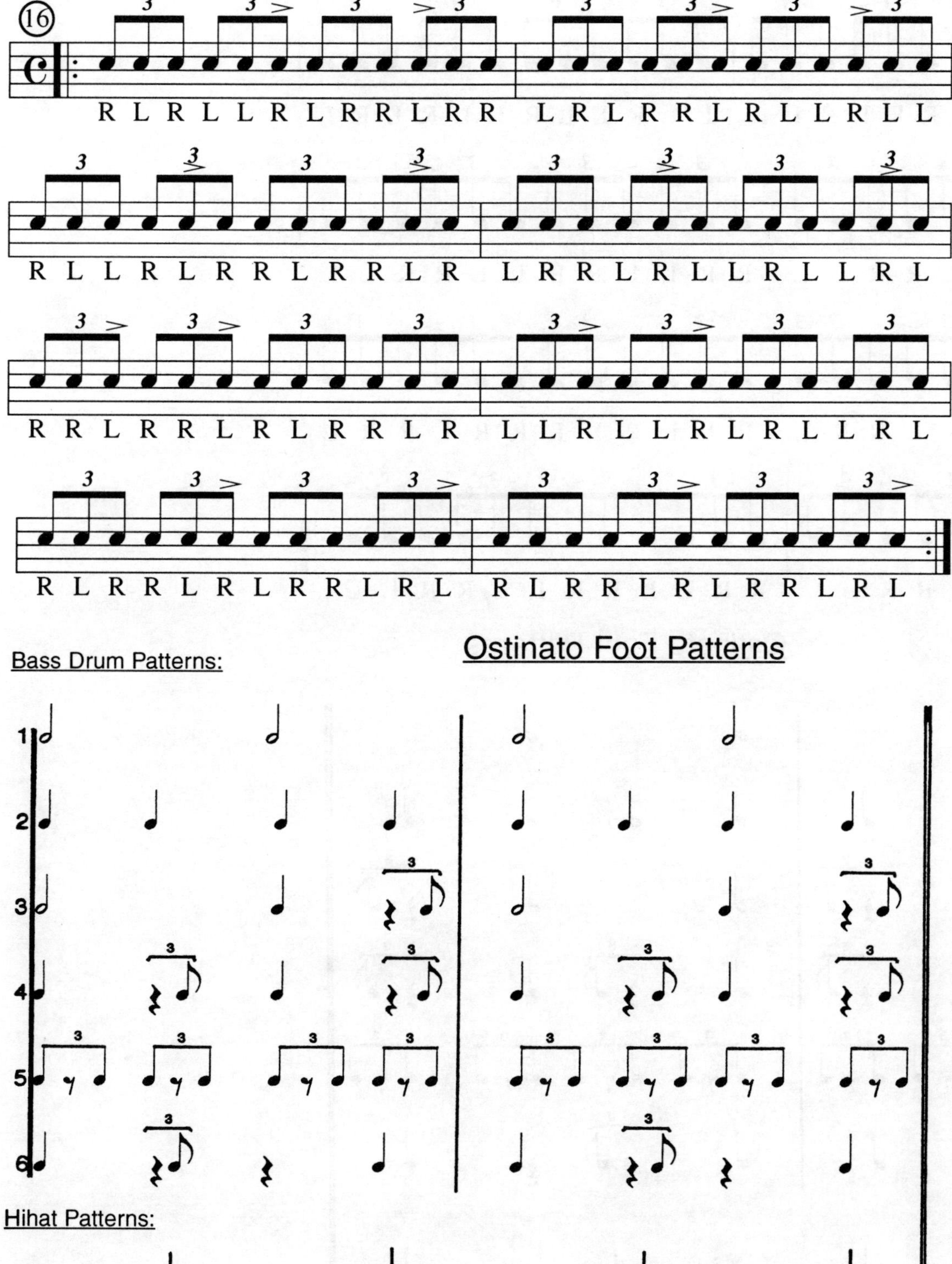

- Feel free to pencil in the different ostinato (constant) bass drum patterns on the lowest space in the staff, for the 8 bar hand solo located above.
- One may also choose and pencil in a desired hihat foot pattern.

Swiss Army Triplet/Mixed Sticking Study

Part C

- Feel free to pencil in the different ostinato (constant) bass drum patterns on the lowest space in the staff, for the 8 bar hand solo located above.
- One may also choose and pencil in a desired hihat foot pattern.

Mixed Sticking Study

Part C

- Feel free to pencil in the different ostinato (constant) bass drum patterns on the lowest space in the staff, for the 8 bar hand solo located above.
- One may also choose and pencil in a desired hihat foot pattern.

8 Bar Solos Using 16th Note Rhythms

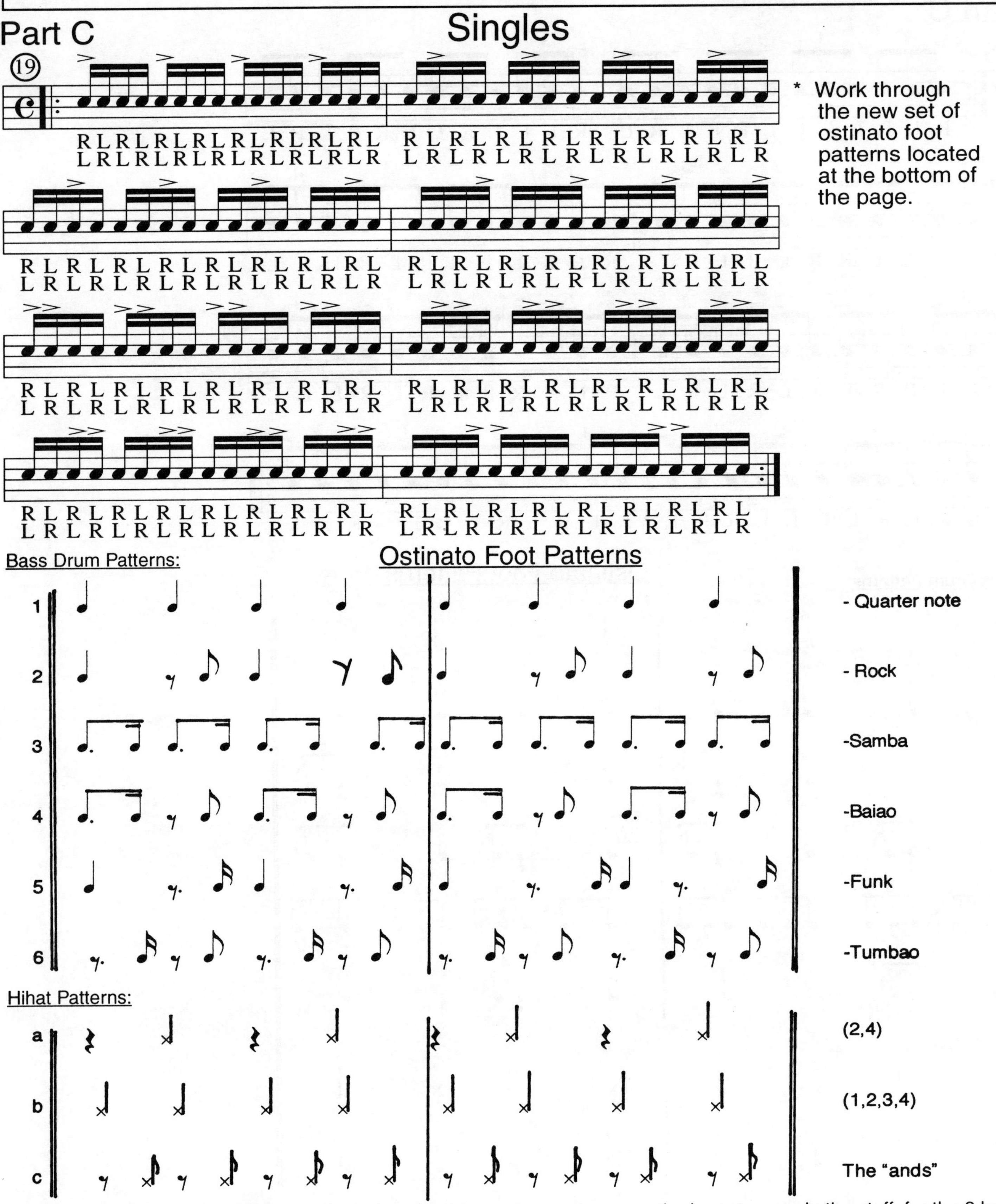

- Feel free to pencil in the different ostinato (constant) bass drum patterns on the lowest space in the staff, for the 8 bar hand solo located above.
- One may also choose and pencil in a desired hihat foot pattern.

Mixed Sticking Study

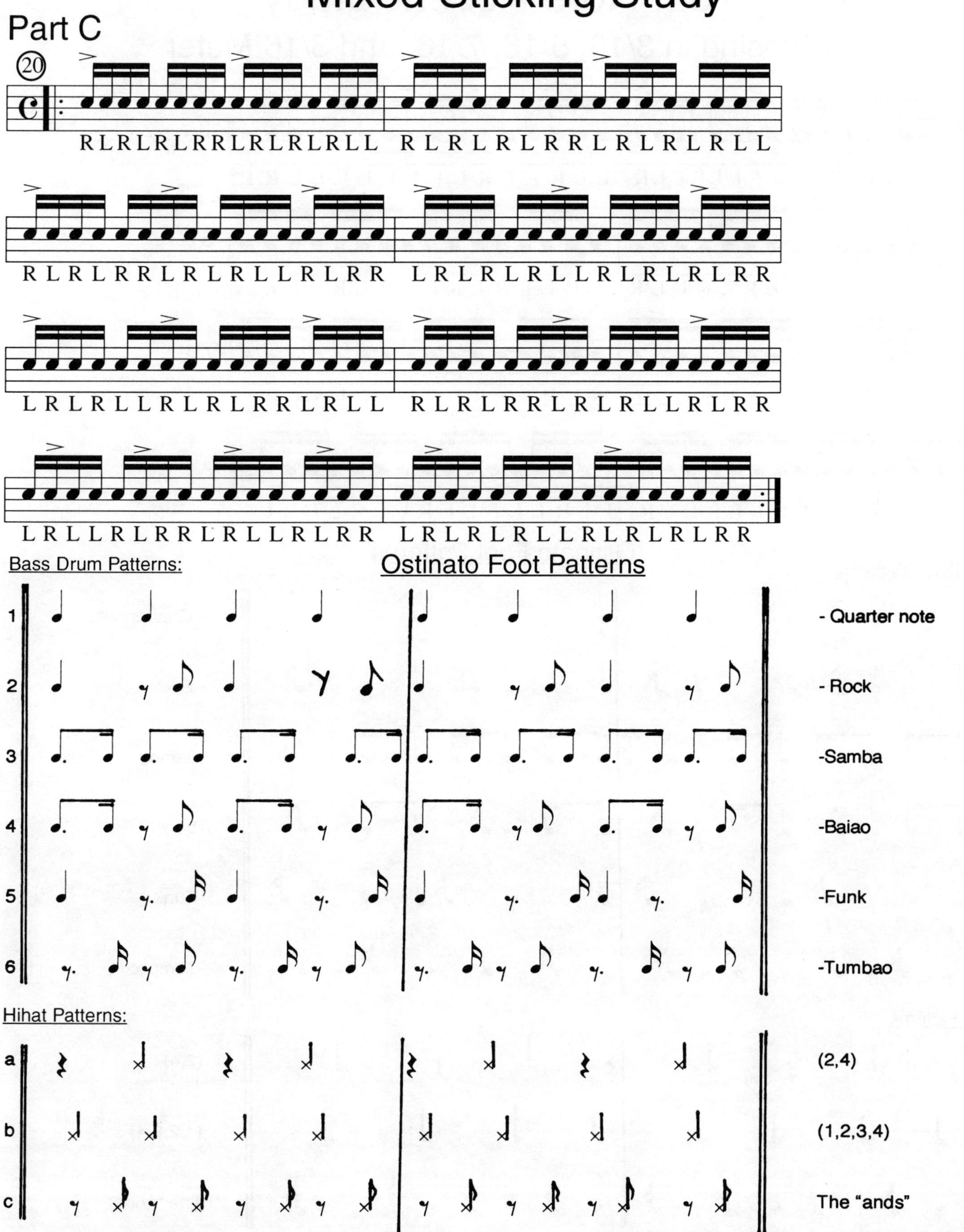

- Feel free to pencil in the different ostinato (constant) bass drum patterns on the lowest space in the staff, for the 8 bar hand solo located above.
- One may also choose and pencil in a desired hihat foot pattern.

16th Note Accent Study

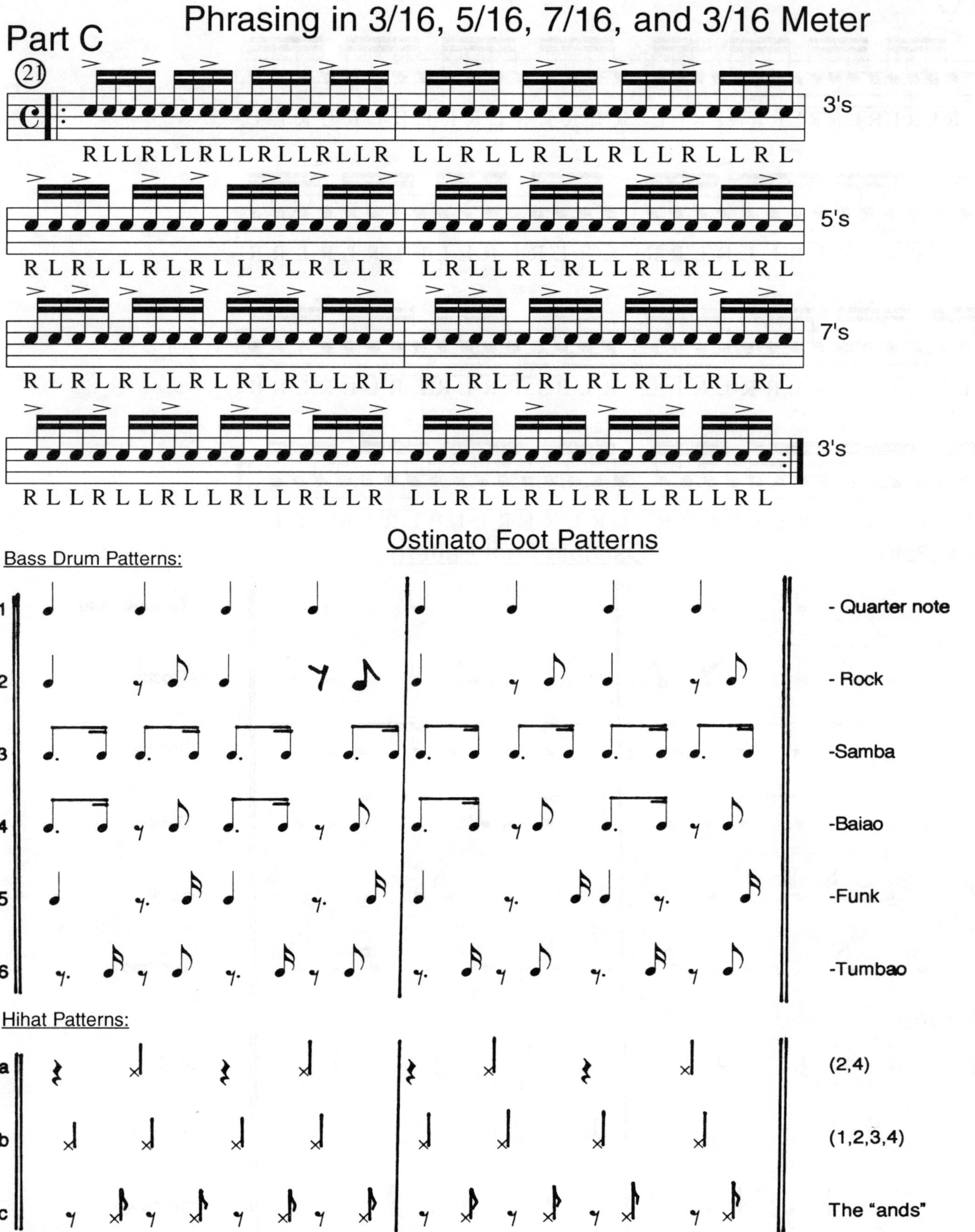

- Feel free to pencil in the different ostinato (constant) bass drum patterns on the lowest space in the staff, for the 8 bar hand solo located above.
- One may also choose and pencil in a desired hihat foot pattern.

Linear Jazz Style (between hands)

The mixed sticking between the ride cymbal and snare helps create a sense of "broken" cymbal time (altering the standard ride cymbal jazz pattern). This also produces more of a progressive jazz sound.

Part D

* R.H. = Ride cymbal
* L.H. = Snare
* For slow to medium tempos swing the eighth notes.
* For uptempos play as written.
* All the 8 bar solos in Part D are derived from the Hand Technique Development solos in Part A.
* The bass drum voicing is played randomly and does not correspond to the written accents in Part A. This was a musical decision.

Linear Jazz Style (continued)

Part D

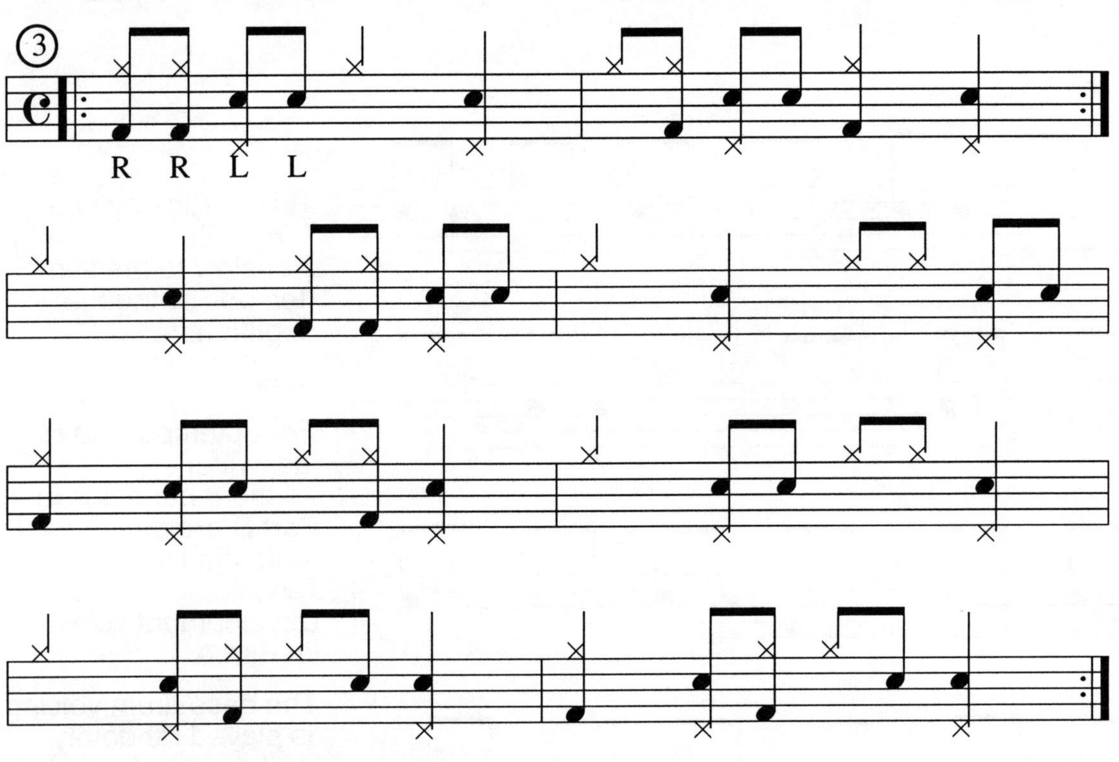

Linear Jazz Style (continued)

Part D

Linear Jazz Style (continued)

Part D

Linear Jazz Style (continued)

Part D

Linear Jazz Style (continued)

Part D

Linear Jazz Style (continued)
8 Bar Solos Using Triplet Rhythms

Part D

Linear Jazz Style (continued)

Part D

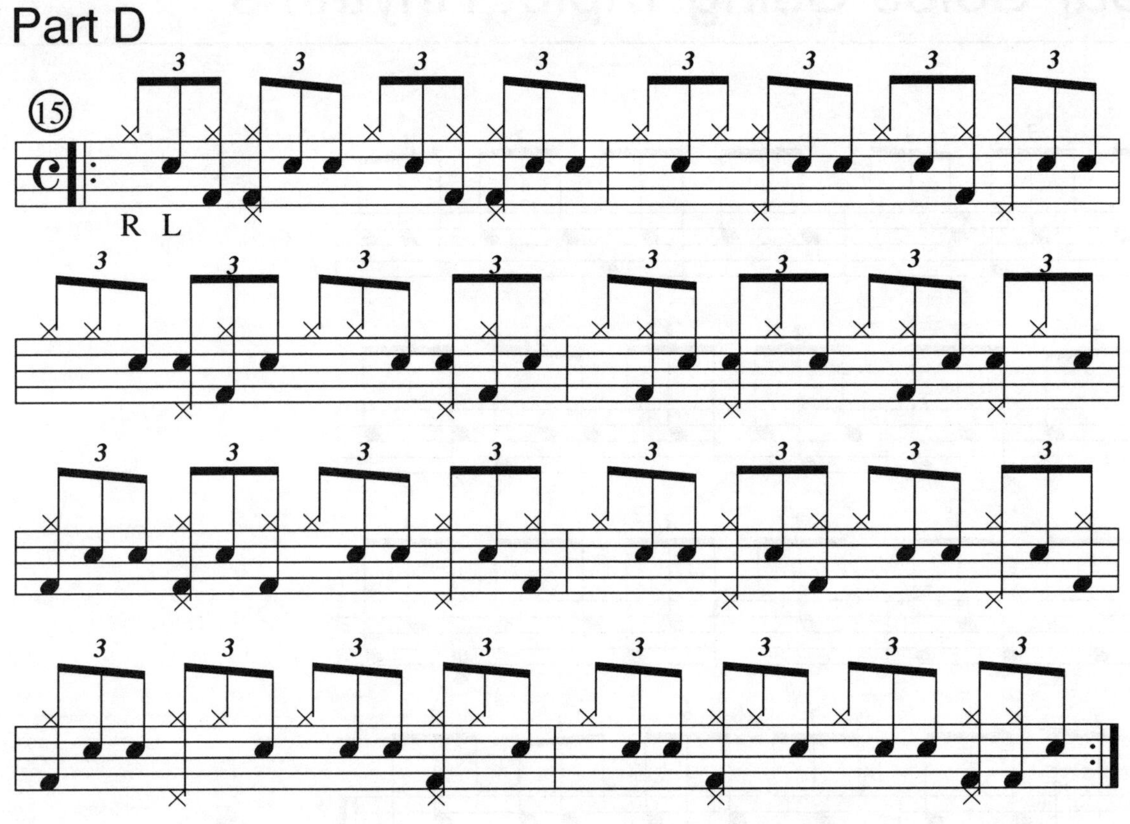

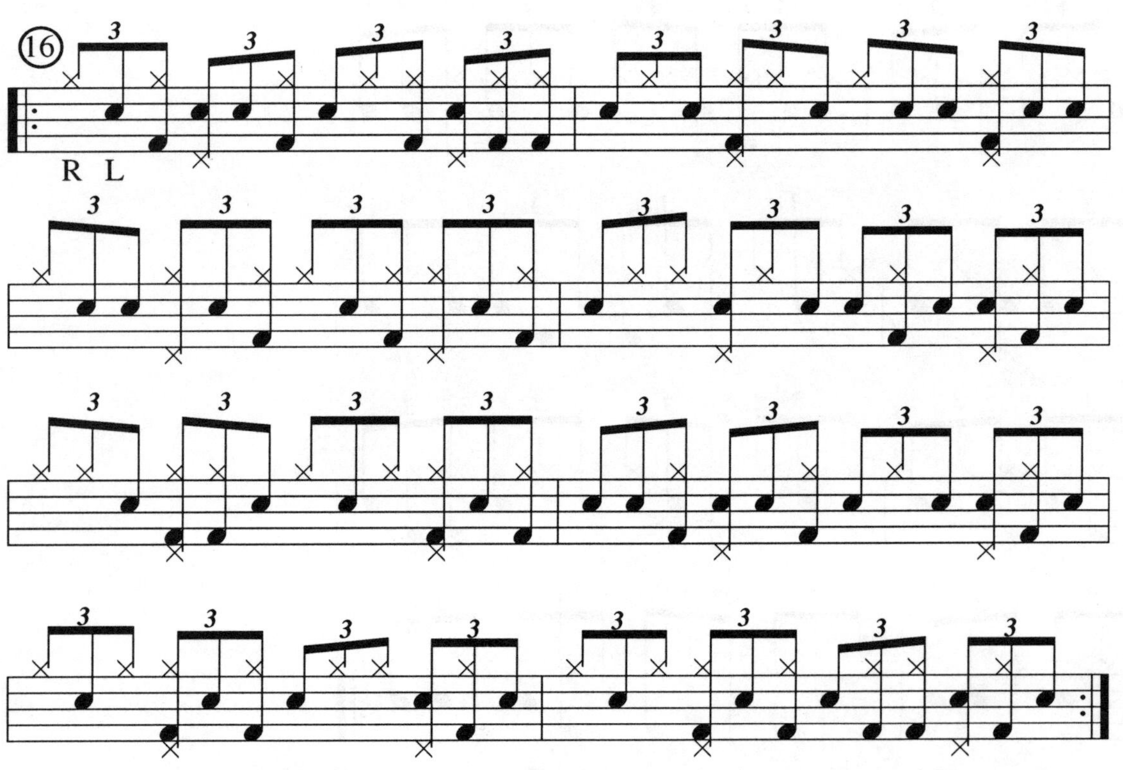

Linear Jazz Style (continued)

Part D

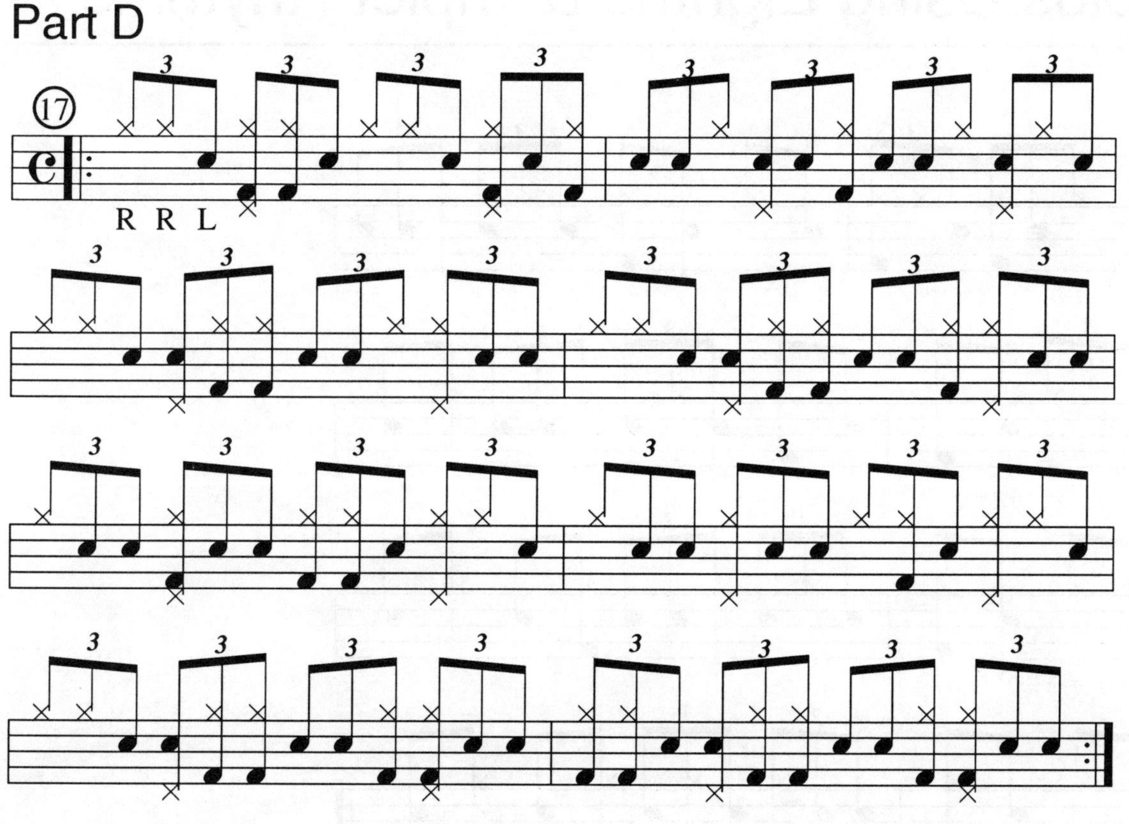

Linear Jazz Style (continued)
8 Bar Solos Using Eighths & Triplet Rhythms

Part D